50 STRATEGIES FOR ACTIVATING YOUR PLC+

50 STRATEGIES FOR ACTIVATING YOUR PLC+

30+ videos including "strategies in action"

Douglas Fisher
Nancy Frey
James Marshall

CORWIN

FOR INFORMATION:

Corwin

A SAGE Company

2455 Teller Road

Thousand Oaks, California 91320

(800) 233-9936

www.corwin.com

SAGE Publications Ltd.

1 Oliver's Yard

55 City Road

London EC1Y 1SP

United Kingdom

SAGE Publications India Pvt. Ltd.

Unit No 323-333, Third Floor, F-Block

International Trade Tower Nehru Place

New Delhi 110 019

India

SAGE Publications Asia-Pacific Pte. Ltd.

18 Cross Street #10-10/11/12

China Square Central

Singapore 048423

Vice President and
  Editorial Director: Monica Eckman

Senior Director and Publisher,
  Content and Product: Lisa Luedeke

Content Development Editor: Sarah Ross

Product Associate, Content
  and Product: Zachary Vann

Production Editor: Tracy Buyan

Copy Editor: Denise McIntyre

Typesetter: C&M Digitals (P) Ltd.

Proofreader: Dennis Webb

Indexer: Integra

Graphic Designer: Gail Buschman

Marketing Manager: Megan Naidl

Copyright © 2026 by Corwin Press, Inc.

All rights reserved. Except as permitted by U.S. copyright law, no part of this work may be reproduced or distributed in any form or by any means, or stored in a database or retrieval system, without permission in writing from the publisher.

When forms and sample documents appearing in this work are intended for reproduction, they will be marked as such. Reproduction of their use is authorized for educational use by educators, local school sites, and/or noncommercial or nonprofit entities that have purchased the book.

All third-party trademarks referenced or depicted herein are included solely for the purpose of illustration and are the property of their respective owners. Reference to these trademarks in no way indicates any relationship with, or endorsement by, the trademark owner.

No AI training. Without in any way limiting the author's and publisher's exclusive rights under copyright, any use of this publication to "train" generative artificial intelligence (AI) or for other AI uses is expressly prohibited. The publisher reserves all rights to license uses of this publication for generative AI training or other AI uses.

Printed and bound by CPI Group (UK) Ltd, Croydon, CR0 4YY

ISBN 9798348810641 (spiral)

Library of Congress Control Number: 2025940839

This book is printed on acid-free paper.

25 26 27 28 29 30 10 9 8 7 6 5 4 3 2 1

DISCLAIMER: This book may direct you to access third-party content via web links, QR codes, or other scannable technologies, which are provided for your reference by the author(s). Corwin makes no guarantee that such third-party content will be available for your use and encourages you to review the terms and conditions of such third-party content. Corwin takes no responsibility and assumes no liability for your use of any third-party content, nor does Corwin approve, sponsor, endorse, verify, or certify such third-party content.

CONTENTS

STRATEGY AND USAGE OVERVIEW	IX
INTRODUCTION	1
The Development of Professional Learning Communities	1
Stepping Into the Activator Role	2
Activators Make Things Happen	3
An Overview of This Guide	5
Your Activation Goal	7
Your Introduction to PLC+ Content Cross-Reference Table	9
50 STRATEGIES FOR ACTIVATING YOUR PLC+	13
Activating Questions 1–5	**15**
1. Activating Question 1: Where are we going?	16
2. Activating Question 2: Where are we now?	20
3. Activating Question 3: How do we move learning forward?	26
4. Activating Question 4: What did we learn today?	30
5. Activating Question 5: Who benefited and who did not benefit?	34
Activator Skills and Abilities	**39**
6. Activator Skills and Abilities: Activating to Achieve a True Impact on Learning	40
7. Activator Skills and Abilities: Assessing Your Activator Fitness Level	42
8. Activator Skills and Abilities: Defining Your Activator Role	46
9. Activator Skills and Abilities: Developing Successful PLC+ Activators	50
10. Activator Skills and Abilities: Facilitation Self-Assessment	54
11. Activator Skills and Abilities: Facilitating With Grace	58
12. Activator Skills and Abilities: Finding the Key Activator	60

Continuous Improvement — 65

13. Continuous Improvement: Discussions and Actions — 66
14. Continuous Improvement: Making Course Corrections — 70
15. Continuous Improvement: Taking Priority Practices to Scale — 74
16. Continuous Improvement: Strong Team Structures to Achieve High Function — 78

Function and Impact — 81

17. Function and Impact: Activating Others by Sharing Your PLC+ Success — 82
18. Function and Impact: Applying Evaluative Thinking — 86
19. Function and Impact: Assessing PLC+ Readiness — 90
20. Function and Impact: Assessing Your Current PLC+ Performance — 94
21. Function and Impact: Building Momentum With Early Wins — 100
22. Function and Impact: Evaluating Your PLC+ Progress and Impact — 102
23. Function and Impact: Increasing Impact in PLC+ Teams — 106
24. Function and Impact: Realizing the Optimal Combination of Function and Impact — 108

Meeting Moves — 111

25. Meeting Moves: Coming to Agreement About Professional Learning — 112
26. Meeting Moves: Documentation and Note-Taking — 114
27. Meeting Moves: Effectively Activating When Meetings Become Challenging — 118
28. Meeting Moves: Establishing Norms — 122
29. Meeting Moves: Establishing PLC+ Roles — 126
30. Meeting Moves: Finding Solid Ground in Assessments and Data — 130
31. Meeting Moves: Social Emotional Check-Ins — 134
32. Meeting Moves: Utilizing Authentic Instructional Protocols — 136

Norms of Collaborative Work — 141

33. Norms of Collaborative Work 1: Pausing — 142
34. Norms of Collaborative Work 2: Paraphrasing — 146
35. Norms of Collaborative Work 3: Posing Questions — 150
36. Norms of Collaborative Work 4: Providing Data — 154
37. Norms of Collaborative Work 5: Putting Ideas on the Table — 158
38. Norms of Collaborative Work 6: Paying Attention to Self and Others — 162
39. Norms of Collaborative Work 7: Presuming Positive Intentions — 166

Team Dynamics — 171

- 40. Team Dynamics: Achieving Team Psychological Safety — 172
- 41. Team Dynamics: Activating Dialogue When Topics Become Sensitive — 176
- 42. Team Dynamics: Activating When Team Members Do Not Want to Change — 178
- 43. Team Dynamics: Analyzing and Describing Team Strengths — 182
- 44. Team Dynamics: Breaking Barriers, Bringing Team Members Together — 186
- 45. Team Dynamics: Countering Resistance With Will, Skill, Knowledge, Capacity, and Emotional Support — 188
- 46. Team Dynamics: From Independent to an Interdependent PLC+ — 192

Time Matters — 197

- 47. Time Matters: Developing an Assessment Calendar — 198
- 48. Time Matters: Scheduling PLC+ Meetings — 204
- 49. Time Matters: Setting Aside Time for the PLC+ — 208

Reflecting on Your Activation of the PLC+ Journey — 211

- 50. Metareflection and Intention Setting With the 5Ds — 212

REFERENCES — 215
INDEX — 217

YOUR WORK AS AN ACTIVATOR JUST GOT EASIER

This book is just the beginning.

Your purchase unlocks access to the PLC+ Activator's Resource Center—an online hub full of tools to help you lead with confidence.

Here's what you'll find:

- Expert Activator Videos—Practical insights from real educators: what worked, what didn't, and how to make each strategy count.
- Ready-to-Use PowerPoints—Strategy highlights you can share directly with your PLC+ team.
- Downloadable, Editable Resources—Customize what you need:
  - Templates (e.g., calendars, meeting notes)
  - Tools (e.g., sample assessments, surveys)
  - Reflection questions to spark discussion
- Curated Links for Deeper Learning—Want to deepen your understanding even further? We've got you covered.

Your PLC+ team is counting on your leadership—and we're with you every step of the way.

Accessing the PLC+ Activator's Resource Center

Visit: https://companion.corwin.com/courses/PLCactivator

Important: Our companion sites now require a free Thinkific account for an improved learning experience. Before accessing the site or scanning QR codes in the book, you'll need to either **create an account** or **log in**.

To ensure smooth access:

- **Create your free Thinkific account** before scanning any QR codes.
- **Check "Remember me"** when logging in to avoid having to sign in repeatedly.
- **Stay logged in** for instant access to all resources.

STRATEGY AND USAGE OVERVIEW

#	Strategy	Page	When to Use			How Often to Use		
			Before Meetings	During Meetings	After Meetings	Planning	Implementation	Reflection
Activating Questions 1–5		15						
1	Activating Question 1: Where are we going?	16		✓			✓	
2	Activating Question 2: Where are we now?	20		✓			✓	
3	Activating Question 3: How do we move learning forward?	26		✓			✓	
4	Activating Question 4: What did we learn today?	30		✓			✓	
5	Activating Question 5: Who benefited and who did not benefit?	34		✓			✓	
Activator Skills and Abilities		39						
6	Activating to Achieve a True Impact on Learning	40		✓			✓	
7	Assessing Your Activator Fitness Level	42	✓			✓		
8	Defining Your Activator Role	46	✓			✓		
9	Developing Successful PLC+ Activators	50	✓			✓		
10	Facilitation Self-Assessment	54	✓			✓		
11	Facilitating With Grace	58		✓			✓	
12	Finding the Key Activator	60	✓			✓		

(Continued)

(Continued)

#	Strategy	Page	When to Use			How Often to Use		
			Before Meetings	During Meetings	After Meetings	Planning	Implementation	Reflection
Continuous Improvement		65						
13	Discussions and Actions	66		✓			✓	
14	Making Course Corrections	70		✓	✓		✓	✓
15	Taking Priority Practices to Scale	74			✓			✓
16	Strong Team Structures to Achieve High Function	78	✓	✓		✓	✓	
Function and Impact		81						
17	Activating Others by Sharing Your PLC+ Success	82			✓		✓	✓
18	Applying Evaluative Thinking	86		✓			✓	✓
19	Assessing PLC+ Readiness	90	✓			✓		
20	Assessing Your Current PLC+ Performance	94			✓		✓	✓
21	Building Momentum With Early Wins	100		✓		✓	✓	
22	Evaluating Your PLC+ Progress and Impact	102			✓		✓	✓
23	Increasing Impact in PLC+ Teams	106		✓			✓	
24	Realizing the Optimal Combination of Function and Impact	108		✓		✓	✓	
Meeting Moves		111						
25	Coming to Agreement About Professional Learning	112		✓			✓	
26	Documentation and Note-Taking	114		✓			✓	
27	Effectively Activating When Meetings Become Challenging	118		✓			✓	
28	Establishing Norms	122		✓		✓	✓	
29	Establishing PLC+ Roles	126		✓		✓		
30	Finding Solid Ground in Assessments and Data	130		✓			✓	
31	Social Emotional Check-Ins	134		✓			✓	
32	Utilizing Authentic Instructional Protocols	136		✓			✓	

#	Strategy	Page	When to Use			How Often to Use		
			Before Meetings	During Meetings	After Meetings	Planning	Implementation	Reflection
Norms of Collaborative Work		141						
33	Pausing	142		✓			✓	
34	Paraphrasing	146		✓			✓	
35	Posing Questions	150		✓			✓	
36	Providing Data	154		✓			✓	
37	Putting Ideas on the Table	158		✓			✓	
38	Paying Attention to Self and Others	162		✓			✓	
39	Presuming Positive Intentions	166		✓			✓	
Team Dynamics		171						
40	Achieving Team Psychological Safety	172		✓			✓	
41	Activating Dialogue When Topics Become Sensitive	176		✓			✓	
42	Activating When Team Members Do Not Want to Change	178		✓			✓	
43	Analyzing and Describing Team Strengths	182		✓			✓	
44	Breaking Barriers, Bringing Team Members Together	186		✓			✓	
45	Countering Resistance With Will, Skill, Knowledge, Capacity, and Emotional Support	188		✓			✓	
46	From Independent to an Interdependent PLC+	192		✓			✓	
Time Matters		197						
47	Developing an Assessment Calendar	198	✓			✓		
48	Scheduling PLC+ Meetings	204	✓			✓		
49	Setting Aside Time for the PLC+	208	✓			✓		
Reflecting on Your Activation of the PLC+ Journey		211						
50	Metareflection and Intention Setting With the 5Ds	212			✓			✓

INTRODUCTION

The PLC+ model relies upon catalysts. These catalysts are people who can successfully move the dialogue from defensiveness and avoidance to decisions and actions that measurably improve teaching and learning: people who can validate and still challenge, who can allow venting but prevent lamenting, and who can ensure a problem-solving and solution-based focus on improving student learning as well as teacher effectiveness and expertise. We call these individuals *activators,* and though they may seem like superhumans, or even superheroes, the leadership they provide is not only possible, but also critical to the success of each team in a PLC+ school. Activators facilitate, but they are far more than facilitators. Activators are true leaders. They press the PLC+ journey forward each step of the way—from establishing goals to taking stock of the current situation—so that *all* students benefit over time.

Welcome to Activating PLC+

qrs.ly/jigpgfz

We encourage you to think about the PLC+ experience as the journey it is. As an activator, you'll be leading that journey. You'll assess needs, note and leverage team members' strengths, design and refine the PLC+ journey, support your colleagues (your fellow travelers) along the way, and adjust the itinerary as needed throughout your journey. Note our emphasis on refining and adjusting. We've never met the perfect PLC+ team or observed a PLC+ journey that didn't have to confront some sort of change during its journey. Let's agree right now that your team, too, will face new challenges, reprioritize outcomes, welcome newly hired team members, and navigate your way through any number of unexpected circumstances. Responsive teams allow for course corrections from the original plan. As an activator, you'll come to expect it, embrace it, exploit it, and share your excitement about it.

THE DEVELOPMENT OF PROFESSIONAL LEARNING COMMUNITIES

Professional learning communities (PLCs) have been a transformative force in education since their inception several decades ago, when they were originally established. The intention was to address the widespread issue of teacher isolation prevalent in the 1950s and 1960s. The foundational idea was that by fostering collaboration among teachers, not only would the educational experience of students be enhanced, but also educators themselves would benefit from being part of a supportive and like-minded network. This collaborative approach has proven to be effective, with robust evidence indicating that well-implemented PLCs significantly enhance teacher practices and student outcomes (e.g., Prenger et al., 2019; Wang & An, 2023).

The success of PLCs hinges on their proper implementation. Over the years, ongoing research and practical experiences have shaped our understanding of what constitutes an effective PLC. This has led to continuous updates in the processes, procedures, and protocols of PLCs, with outdated methods being phased out in favor of new, evidence-based practices. The latest advancement in this evolution is PLC+, a next-generation framework that builds on the legacy of previous models while integrating recent insights into the dynamics of learning communities.

You're likely reading this guide because you've been called upon, selected, or volunteered to fulfill an activator role for your school's PLC+. First, thank you for your leadership! Your contributions will be many, and they will be critical to the PLC+ journey. This guide is the activator's companion to the core PLC+ guide, *Your Introduction to PLC+* (Fisher & Frey, 2025). Together, these resources will support you and your team as you prepare for what lies ahead.

But how will all of this happen? How do you ensure that the PLC+ team and its efforts are intentional, relevant, and successful? And how, over time, will you make sure the effort evolves, improves, and exacts to achieve the transformative promise that the research indicates a PLC+ is capable of achieving? Reaching these outcomes relies on leadership. That is the role you've been called to fill: the role of PLC+ activator.

Strong activation is essential for success in all PLC+ settings. Many previous PLC models and frameworks disregarded the role human behavior plays when it comes to collaborative efforts to impact student learning at high levels. The PLC+ framework considers this critical element of human behavior on a deep level, with activation as one of its crosscutting values. Through their intentional and informed leadership, activators move the PLC+ team from chaos and dysfunction into impactful action—from where team members are stagnant to where they thrive. Activators ensure that their teams' PLC+ journeys are focused on the learning and development of the adults involved and the students they teach. In doing so, activators lead their teams to weather the storms that may appear, to overcome the inevitable challenges they will face, and to celebrate their individual and collective successes.

We wrote this guide to support the activators on whom PLC+ relies. Likely, you're reading this book in preparation for this critical role. Mark Lawrence (2017), in his book *Red Sister*, observed, "A book is as dangerous as any journey you might take. The person who closes the back cover may not be the same one that opened the front one. Treat them with respect" (p. 103). When readers implement the tools presented throughout **50 Strategies for Activating Your PLC+**, the experience can be life changing; we have witnessed this happen in PLC+ teams more times than we can count. With that in mind, we encourage you to treat this journey with the respect it requires, as you anticipate the amazing transformations that can result for yourself, your colleagues, and your students.

STEPPING INTO THE ACTIVATOR ROLE

Successful leaders begin by understanding their role and responsibilities. They also take in the current situation as a starting point, while scanning the horizon for needs and opportunities—essentially exploring various destinations that could become the

PLC+ focus. This guide will support you in your leadership role and responsibility for implementing PLC+ with your team. Although this guide is designed specifically to support you in the activator's role, *Your Introduction to PLC+* contains additional resources to support each member's contributions to the PLC+.

If you're unfamiliar with the PLC+ concept, start by reading *Your Introduction to PLC+* (Fisher & Frey, 2025). Then, keep that book close for easy reference as you continue with this guide. We encourage you to take notes, mark up pages and passages, or grab a pad of sticky notes to accomplish the same. Your background knowledge should include the following key concepts from the PLC+ model:

- The five guiding questions
- The four crosscutting values
- The role of the common challenge
- Liberatory design

The exploration of the five guiding questions prompts action, and teams use specific protocols to implement their plan (see Figure i.1). Essentially, as PLC+ teams collaborate to find solutions to these questions, they create a sophisticated network of thoughts and actions that enhance the entire educational experience—for teachers and students alike. The following PLC+ model illustrates this vision.

Figure i.1: The PLC+ Model

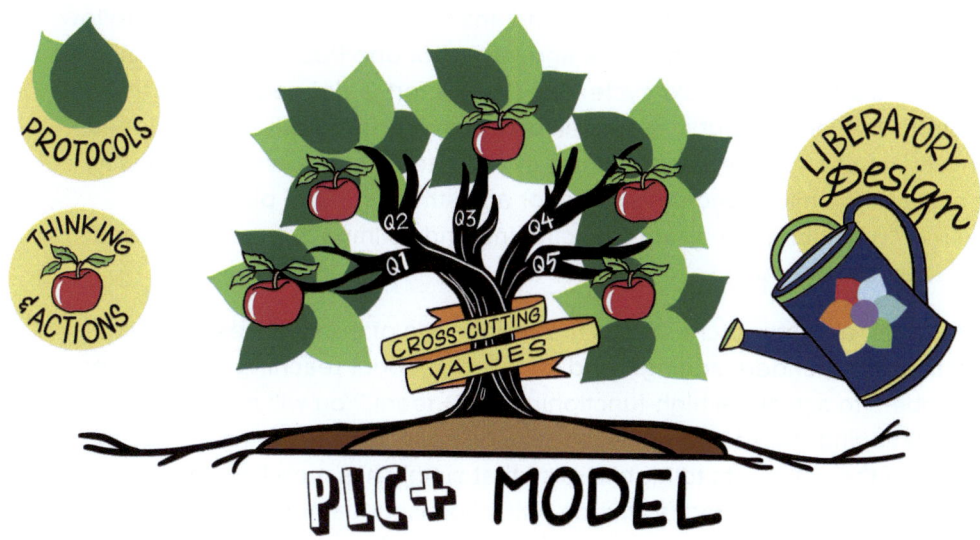

Source: Fisher, D., & Frey, N. (2025). *Your introduction to PLC+*. Corwin.

ACTIVATORS MAKE THINGS HAPPEN

We have described and begun to define the term *activator* as applied to PLC+. As an activator, you're the lead planner, lead implementer, lead motivator and cheerleader, and lead celebrant when goals are met and impact is realized. Let's dive a bit deeper into the activator role and your calling to walk in activator shoes.

Activation is more than facilitation. Facilitating a meeting suggests a hierarchy and places the responsibility on a single individual. Whether intentional or not, this arrangement opens the door for divesting other PLC+ members of ownership. That, in most ways, is the exact opposite of what a PLC+ should be.

Beginning with the end in mind, and informed by the thousands of PLC+ teams we've led and observed, we suggest that effective activators possess and act on the following:

- High credibility among their colleagues and students
- An ability to lead adults in their learning process
- The desire to effectively support and challenge the team members, their colleagues, and themselves
- The belief that all students and all teachers can learn at high levels
- The commitment to demonstrate resilience in times of challenge
- An ability to lead the PLC+ work, monitoring and adjusting it along the way

Many of the strategies we will share serve to foster and support these skills, abilities, and aptitudes. But the last point—the ability to monitor and adjust—begs elaboration. PLC+ activators serve as leaders for a systematic effort in which the outputs of one element become inputs for the next. It's systematic because teams use the answers to the first guiding question (your "output") as an "input" toward answering the next guiding question, and so on across the full set of five guiding questions to inform the work and answers to the questions that follow. It's also systemic because the work and impact of one PLC+ investigation cycle is designed to support the next cycle. The PLC+ effort is defined, in part, through the activator's leadership. But it should also involve a collaboratively developed plan with input and agreement among all PLC+ team members. Additionally, the activator monitors and advocates for adjustments to the plan, when required, to heighten the team's functioning and its impact on students and PLC+ team members.

A successful activator orchestrates the wide range of experiences, specific expertise, skills, understandings, and knowledge about teaching and learning of members to achieve a high-functioning PLC+ team. You will not find a high-functioning PLC+ team—one driving the learning of its members and the learning of their students to high levels—that simply has meetings facilitated by an appointed or nominated facilitator. Activation is fundamentally different: as an activator, you are crucial in making sure your group is successful. Having a plan to collaboratively manage the structural elements of your PLC+ is critical.

Ultimately, as the leader, you want the team to benefit from each team member's contributions. Successful activators not only lead the PLC+ team and effort, but also bring out the leadership abilities of their team members. We've suggested that successful activators are extraordinary in certain ways. Yet it is far from necessary to be superhuman to qualify for the role. To serve in this critical leadership role, you just need the skills, abilities, and dispositions outlined in this guide.

AN OVERVIEW OF THIS GUIDE

This guide contains the concrete structures and actions activators can use to lead the PLC+ journey. As an activator, your leadership role is as an agent who moves the substance of the dialogue purposefully toward more effective teaching and learning. Although we believe the activator will be the individual leading the team, it's an important feature of the PLC+ framework that everyone on the team can serve as the activator at certain times to ensure that learning is moving forward for the adults and for our students. We are also aware that teams will engage in the PLC+ framework at different stages and have different leadership needs based on their experience collaborating, the time and resources they have available, and so on. Ultimately, however, we are all moving toward a common goal: effective PLC+ teams that impact teaching and learning.

We have organized the fifty strategies useful for activators into eight categories. These categories are presented as follows:

1. **Activating Questions 1–5.** The strategies in this first section focus on the PLC+ questions themselves and strategies activators can use to engage team members in robust conversations. The five guiding questions can be used in any order based on what the team needs to accomplish in a given session; often, several questions are discussed in the same meeting. The strategies in this section provide activators with potential responses to challenges that may arise as teams interact.

2. **Activator Skills and Abilities.** There are specific skills activators need to support their teams to engage in the work of a PLC+. These skills range from self-assessing your personal fitness for activation to defining your role as an activator to basic facilitation skills. Yes, activators do facilitate, but they do much more than that. This section provides the foundation for activators as they engage in their work.

3. **Continuous Improvement.** As activators engage in supporting their teams, they are on the lookout for opportunities to make improvements in their systems and organization. The strategies in this section provide support for activators to recognize the need to improve and to make course corrections in real time. In addition, the strategies in this section help activators build stronger and stronger teams.

4. **Function and Impact.** This section includes tools and strategies that activators can use to assess their team's readiness for PLC+ work as well as the current performance of their teams. In addition, there are strategies that allow teams to recognize their wins and systematically increase their impact. The goal of this section is to create high-functioning teams that have a strong impact on teachers and students.

5. **Meeting Moves.** This section focuses on the implementation of the meeting discussions themselves. Of course, PLCs are more than meetings. Yet meetings, and effective discussions during those sessions, are a critical dimension of the PLC+ model. Activators need tools that support the discussions that team members have, from establishing norms to using protocols to documenting their conversations.

6. **Norms of Collaborative Work.** As part of the conversations that teams have, activators play a special role in creating the norms for conversations. The strategies in this section, adopted and adapted from *Cognitive Coaching* (Costa & Garmston, 2015), have been tested for decades. They provide activators with tools they can use to support effective collaborative work that PLC+ teams do each time they meet.

7. **Team Dynamics.** As humans, we have social relations—thus, various dynamics operate as we interact. Activators recognize these dynamics and use tools to ensure that team members experience psychological safety and relational trust. In addition, activators focus on team members' strengths and foster interdependence within their teams. In fact, strong team dynamics allow members to focus on the work because they develop a strong sense of belonging to the team.

8. **Time Matters.** The final section focuses on some of the logistics that activators must attend to, such as developing an assessment calendar or scheduling times for teams to meet. These logistics ensure that teams have the organizational support they need to complete their work. Without these supports, teams start to focus their time on logistics rather than impacting learning.

We have also indicated the point or points in your PLC+ effort when each strategy is most likely to be used. We encourage you to be informed by that designation, but certainly not entrapped. You may find a particular strategy is useful at points beyond our "most likely" designation.

Here are some suggestions about how you might best use this guide based on your current understanding of PLC+ and the activator role, as well as your point in the PLC+ journey.

I want to	How to Proceed
Build my understanding of the entire PLC+ planning and implementation process	Proceed in the traditional way by reading this guide front to back. Enjoy the many examples to help you picture PLC+ in action. Highlight and make notes about how the guidance and ideas will influence your leadership of your PLC+. Take note of tools you can turn to when the time is right across the implementation journey.
Get support for a particular point in the PLC+ journey	Take stock of your current point in the PLC+ journey. Then, jump into the corresponding part of this guide. As you review the content and guidance, record key things you'll be especially mindful about and key steps you plan to take. Take time to describe the strengths of your PLC+ team where they intersect with the implementation work you're leading. Finally, think about any challenges you're likely to encounter, and plan your approach to avoid, address, or accept them—should they arise.

I want to	How to Proceed
Refresh my memory about a specific task right before implementing it with my team	With the particular task or process in mind, use the Table of Contents or Index to pinpoint the resource or resources available to you for the specific task you face. Spend some time reviewing what you find and envisioning the implementation work with your team. Picture the ideal process and outcome and press yourself to define what is necessary for that ideal to become a reality. Now, anticipate what could get in the way of achieving the same outcome and have a strategy or strategies ready—should they be needed.

To support your use of this guide, we've included a cross-reference table that links each of the 50 strategies to related content in the foundational text, *Your Introduction to PLC+*. This resource makes it easy to locate additional context and guidance for any strategy that piques your interest. You'll find the table beginning on page 9.

> This guide was written for currently serving activators and those with aspirations to serve. It will also be used by school leaders in the natural course of supporting the PLC+ and activators in their schools. When you encounter forward-looking strategies, such as strategies for selecting an activator, consider the following:
>
> - If you're an activator, remember there is always room for more. Use the guidance to identify additional, high-potential peers who can prepare for the activator role.
>
> - If you're a leader, use the guidance to inform your search for ideal activators to support your PLC+ effort.

YOUR ACTIVATION GOAL

In the final module of *Your Introduction to PLC+*, we noted the importance of developing collective effervescence for teams. *Collective effervescence* is a term coined by French sociologist Émile Durkheim more than a hundred years ago. It's that feeling of energy, joy, and harmony that comes when people are engaged in a shared purpose. But it starts with collective responsibility. As you recall from *Your Introduction to PLC+*, the key elements of collective responsibility include the following (Hirsch, 2010):

- All staff members share a commitment to the success of each student.

- Educators do not allow any single teacher to fail in their attempt to ensure the success of any one student.

- Students benefit from the wisdom and expertise of all teachers, rather than just of the teachers to whom they are assigned.
- Teachers willingly share with their colleagues what is working in their classrooms.
- Teachers with less experience realize that other teachers are invested in their success and the success of all students.

Collective responsibility can take many forms, but we recognize it when we hear teams talking about their students as *our* students, not as *your* students and *my* students. You will recognize it when you see team members sharing ideas and supporting colleagues, even offering to collaborate in teaching. Activators have the potential to foster collective responsibility as they support team members to make decisions collaboratively, to see *all* the students as their students, and to ensure that all students benefit from all teachers.

Some teams move beyond collective responsibility to collective efficacy. *Collective efficacy*, which has been extensively studied, has a strong influence on learning (Eells, 2011). Collective efficacy is a belief—specifically, a belief that a group of people have the power to achieve their goals. They understand that, together, they can make a difference. Importantly, that belief must be fed by evidence for efficacy to develop. Like collective responsibility, collective efficacy can take many forms, but you recognize it when you hear teams engaged in goal setting through their common challenge and when you see teams taking actions to achieve their goals, collect evidence of their impact, and revise their actions to achieve their goal. We have never encountered a team with high levels of collective efficacy that did not also demonstrate collective responsibility. In fact, collective responsibility is a prerequisite to collective efficacy. Activators can support teams to move from collective responsibility to collective efficacy by helping them set goals, collect evidence, and determine their impact. Celebrating wins and success also fosters collective efficacy.

Some teams move beyond collective efficacy to *collective effervescence* and genuinely experience joy from the work they do together. They look forward to time with their team, and they experience great success in their collaborative efforts. We've never met a team with collective effervescence that did not have collective efficacy. Teams that have collective responsibility, collective efficacy, and collective effervescence have an impact, work in harmony, look forward to their time together, and reap the rewards of teaching. That's why activators aim to help each PLC+ develop these collectives: responsibility, efficacy, and effervescence.

YOUR INTRODUCTION TO PLC+ CONTENT CROSS-REFERENCE TABLE

This table supports readers in cross-referencing strategies and foundational content from *Your Introduction to PLC+*. Each of the 50 strategies in this guide has been matched to the primary module or section in the foundational text for easy reference.

Strategy #	Title	Section	Related Concept From *Your Introduction to PLC+*	Module/Page(s)
1	Where Are We Going?	Activating Questions 1–5	Guiding Question 1: Teacher Clarity, Learning Intentions, Success Criteria	Module 1 (pp. 49–73)
2	Where Are We Now?	Activating Questions 1–5	Guiding Question 2: Strengths-Based Data Use, Initial Assessments, Focal Students	Module 2 (pp. 75–91)
3	How Do We Move Learning Forward?	Activating Questions 1–5	Guiding Question 3: Evidence-Based Instruction, Learning Phases	Module 3 (pp. 101–127)
4	What Did We Learn Today?	Activating Questions 1–5	Guiding Question 4: Reflection and Evidence Analysis	Module 4 (pp. 131–162)
5	Who Benefited and Who Did Not Benefit?	Activating Questions 1–5	Guiding Question 5: Equity, Disaggregated Data	Module 5 (pp. 165–194)
6	Activating to Achieve a True Impact on Learning	Activator Skills and Abilities	Crosscutting Values: High Expectations, Evidence-Based Practice	Module 3
7	Assessing Your Activator Fitness Level	Activator Skills and Abilities	Activator Role and Self-Assessment	Module 6; Intro (pp. 1–48)
8	Defining Your Activator Role	Activator Skills and Abilities	Activator Dispositions, Crosscutting Value: Activation	Introduction (pp. 5–8); Module 6
9	Developing Successful PLC+ Activators	Activator Skills and Abilities	Credibility, Growth Mindset, Resilience	Intro; Module 6
10	Facilitation Self-Assessment	Activator Skills and Abilities	Facilitation for Equity and Inclusion	Module 6 (pp. 197–228)
11	Facilitating With Grace	Activator Skills and Abilities	Liberatory Design, Psychological Safety	Module 6
12	Finding the Key Activator	Activator Skills and Abilities	Shared Leadership; Role Clarity	Introduction; Module 6
13	Discussions and Actions	Continuous Improvement	Monitoring, Reflection, PLC+ Cycles	Module 6 (pp. 197–228)

(Continued)

(Continued)

#	Strategy Title	Section	Related Concept From *Your Introduction to PLC+*	Module/Page(s)
14	Making Course Corrections	Continuous Improvement	Real-Time Data Use, Instructional Adjustment	Modules 4 & 6
15	Taking Priority Practices to Scale	Continuous Improvement	Scaling, Adaptive Leadership	Modules 5–6
16	Strong Team Structures to Achieve High Function	Continuous Improvement	Collaboration Norms, Role Distribution	Module 6
17	Activating Others by Sharing Your PLC+ Success	Function and Impact	Storytelling, Stakeholder Communication	Module 6
18	Applying Evaluative Thinking	Function and Impact	Inquiry, Evidence Analysis, Adjustment	Modules 4 & 6
19	Assessing PLC+ Readiness	Function and Impact	Readiness Assessment Tool	Module 6 (pp. 205–228)
20	Assessing Your Current PLC+ Performance	Function and Impact	Self-Assessment Against 5 Guiding Questions	Module 6
21	Building Momentum With Early Wins	Function and Impact	Momentum Building; Short-Term Goal Setting; Collective Efficacy	Module 6
22	Evaluating Your PLC+ Progress and Impact	Function and Impact	Progress Monitoring; Data-Informed Decision Making	Module 6
23	Increasing Impact in PLC+ Teams	Function and Impact	Collaborative Practice; Trust; Protocols for Reflection	Module 6
24	Realizing the Optimal Combination of Function and Impact	Function and Impact	MacDonald's Framework; High Functioning + High Impact Teams	Modules 5–6
25	Coming to Agreement About Professional Learning	Meeting Moves	Adult Learning; Shared Vision; Resistance Management	Module 6
26	Documentation and Note-Taking	Meeting Moves	Team Documentation; Meeting Artifacts; AI Support Tools	Module 6
27	Effectively Activating When Meetings Become Challenging	Meeting Moves	Liberatory Design; Psychological Safety; Equity Conversations	Module 6
28	Establishing Norms	Meeting Moves	Team Agreements; Norms of Collaborative Work	Module 6
29	Establishing PLC+ Roles	Meeting Moves	Distributed Leadership; Clear Role Assignment	Module 6
30	Finding Solid Ground in Assessments and Data	Meeting Moves	Assessment Literacy; Data Dialogues; Triangulation	Modules 2 & 4

#	Title	Section	Related Concept From *Your Introduction to PLC+*	Module/Page(s)
31	Social Emotional Check-Ins	Meeting Moves	Psychological Safety; Emotional Regulation; Equity-Centered Practice	Module 6
32	Utilizing Authentic Instructional Protocols	Meeting Moves	Purpose-Driven Protocol Use; Guiding Questions	Modules 1–5
33	Pausing	Norms of Collaborative Work	Cognitive Coaching; Wait Time; Conversational Equity	Module 6
34	Paraphrasing	Norms of Collaborative Work	Communication Clarity; Active Listening	Module 6
35	Posing Questions	Norms of Collaborative Work	Inquiry Mindset; Reflective Thinking; Cognitive Coaching	Modules 3 & 6
36	Providing Data	Norms of Collaborative Work	Evidence-Informed Reflection; Data Conversations; Equity	Modules 2, 4 & 6
37	Putting Ideas on the Table	Norms of Collaborative Work	Collaboration Safety; Neutral Language; Collective Ownership	Module 6
38	Paying Attention to Self and Others	Norms of Collaborative Work	Social Sensitivity; Emotional Awareness; Meeting Culture	Module 6
39	Presuming Positive Intentions	Norms of Collaborative Work	Reframing Dialogue; Team Norms; Trust Building	Module 6
40	Achieving Team Psychological Safety	Team Dynamics	Trust; Inclusion; Psychological Safety Stages	Module 6
41	Activating Dialogue When Topics Become Sensitive	Team Dynamics	Liberatory Design; Courageous Conversations; Equity Reflection	Module 6
42	Activating When Team Members Do Not Want to Change	Team Dynamics	Change Resistance; Trust; Accountability	Module 6
43	Analyzing and Describing Team Strengths	Team Dynamics	Strengths-Based Culture; Team Assessment; Clarity in Roles	Module 6
44	Breaking Barriers, Bringing Team Members Together	Team Dynamics	Belonging; Shared Purpose; Relational Trust	Modules 5 & 6
45	Countering Resistance With Will, Skill, Knowledge, Capacity, & Emotional Support	Team Dynamics	Coaching; Differentiated Adult Learning; Adaptive Support	Module 6
46	From Independent to an Interdependent PLC+	Team Dynamics	Collective Efficacy; Shared Leadership; Systemic Alignment	Modules 5 & 6

(Continued)

(Continued)

Strategy #	Title	Section	Related Concept From *Your Introduction to PLC+*	Module/Page(s)
47	Developing an Assessment Calendar	Time Matters	Assessment Planning; Coherence Across Units	Module 6
48	Scheduling PLC+ Meetings	Time Matters	Structural Planning; Team Coordination	Module 6
49	Setting Aside Time for the PLC+	Time Matters	Strategic Time Use; Organizational Support	Module 6
50	Metareflection and Intention Setting With the 5Ds	Reflecting on Your Activation	Metareflection; PLC+ Impact; Liberatory Design	Modules 5–6

50 Strategies for Activating Your PLC+

ACTIVATING QUESTIONS 1-5

An Introduction to Questions 1–5

qrs.ly/u8gpgg2

1. ACTIVATING QUESTION 1: WHERE ARE WE GOING?

What strategies can address challenges that arise when activating PLC+ Question 1?					
When					
	Before Meetings	✓	During Meetings		After Meetings
How Often					
	Planning	✓	Implementation		Reflection

Strategy in Action | Activating Question 1: Where Are We Going?

qrs.ly/gygpgg3

STRATEGY-AT-A-GLANCE

The question "Where are we going?" is often the entry point for PLC+ investigation cycles. This question focuses attention on making the intentions for learning explicit. It challenges teams to make clear, intentional decisions about the learning path they will take.

Activators should be ready to navigate challenges that arise from disagreements about standards or from difficulties in developing learning intentions, success criteria, and learning progressions.

RECOGNIZING THE NEED

The fifth-grade team at Juarez Elementary begins by asking, "Where are we going?" to anchor the planning that happens in their weekly PLC+ team meeting. They dive deep to identify the essential learning outcomes for their upcoming unit on fractions. The team collaborates to define what success looks like for students and then maps out intentional steps to get there. This clarity helps them design more purposeful instruction that aligns with student needs and learning goals.

ACTIVATING WITH THIS STRATEGY

As your PLC+ team engages with this first guiding question, members will define the learning intentions, success criteria, and learning progressions—referred to by some of our Canadian colleagues as *curriculum expectations*—that are aligned with the standards set by their state or province, district, and school. Common barriers often emerge when teams ask, "Where are we going?" By identifying and examining these potential challenges early on, teams can be better prepared to address—or even prevent—the most frequent obstacles to progress.

The challenges we have identified below are drawn from our experiences working with districts, schools, and classrooms around the world. We have also found that when we look beyond how a barrier initially presents itself and then seek to understand its underlying cause, the path toward resolution becomes clearer. After reviewing the barriers we've outlined, take time to reflect on your own PLC+ team. Consider the challenges you might face and begin to imagine strategies for overcoming them.

Paving the Way to Activating Question 1: Where are we going?			
Potential Challenges When Activating Question 1	**Possible Reasons**	**Ways to Address and Overcome**	**Discussion Starters and Questions**
The PLC+ identifies too many standards to analyze.	The activator and the team may be trying to "teach everything" rather than focusing on the essential skills, knowledge, and understandings—leaving members with a perceived expectation to teach them all in a small amount of time.	Activators can lead the team in the right direction by ensuring that the team takes time to analyze specific standards being considered for an investigation cycle.	"Let's analyze all three of these standards one at a time. I will project them on the screen, and we can do these together to identify what concepts and skills are common in all of them."
The PLC+ team is struggling with the development of learning intentions, success criteria, and learning progressions.	Ensuring "teacher clarity"—including learning progressions, learning intentions, and success criteria—is a different way of looking at teaching and learning, whereas the team may be using a traditional approach. For example, the current approach to clarity may be the traditional method of writing standards or "The student will be able to . . ." system.	Develop a professional learning library of resources and examples of learning intentions, success criteria, and learning progressions.	"Let's build our learning intentions, success criteria, and progressions together as a PLC+. We'll get better with practice." "Are there essential vocabulary terms we need to clarify for students?" "Are there any missing skills or concepts that might prevent access to this standard?"

Your Additional Challenges and Strategies to Overcome			
Additional Challenges When Activating Question 1	**Possible Reasons for This Challenge**	**Ways You Will Address and Overcome**	**Discussion Starters and Questions**

SUCCESS CHECKLIST

✓	Activation Task
	Note Potential Challenges
☐	The PLC+ team disagrees on which standards to analyze.
☐	The team identifies too many standards to analyze.
☐	The team struggles to develop learning intentions, success criteria, and learning progressions.
	Activate
☐	Analyze specific standards for upcoming units and list concepts/skills to ensure focus.
☐	Develop a professional learning library with resources and examples of clarity elements.
☐	Anticipate challenges your PLC+ might encounter as you work to answer the first PLC+ question and identify the solutions you'll employ in advance.
	Reflect and Refine
☐	Are the correct standards being prioritized, and to what extent are personal preferences unduly influencing the process?
☐	On a continuum running from "covering everything" to "focusing on the essentials," is the current work focused on essentials?
☐	How can your PLC+ approach to developing clear learning intentions and criteria be continuously strengthened to make your PLC+ team more efficient and effective?

Notes

2. ACTIVATING QUESTION 2: WHERE ARE WE NOW?

What strategies can address challenges that arise when activating PLC+ Question 2?					
When					
	Before Meetings	✓	During Meetings		After Meetings
How Often					
	Planning	✓	Implementation		Reflection

Strategy in Action | Activating Question 2: Where Are We Now?

qrs.ly/1rgpgg5

STRATEGY-AT-A-GLANCE

Question 2 can surface underlying biases about student learning and specific groups of students. Effectively navigating this question requires an awareness of these biases and the ability to recognize when they influence PLC+ team discussions. Activators should be prepared to address not only the challenges that stem from bias, but also those that arise when student work is not analyzed, common assessments are underused, interpretations of data vary, or student perspectives are excluded from the PLC+ process.

RECOGNIZING THE NEED

During a PLC+ meeting at Middletown High, the ninth-grade algebra team reviews preassessment data to determine students' readiness for solving linear equations. One teacher is surprised to see that students from a typically underperforming subgroup scored among the highest, challenging some long-held assumptions. The team realizes they had been unintentionally planning remediation for students who didn't need it, based on past performance rather than current evidence. This moment prompts a deeper reflection on their own biases and reinforces the importance of using authentic student data to drive instruction.

ACTIVATING WITH THIS STRATEGY

Once learning intentions, success criteria, and learning progressions have been established, PLC+ teams can begin the initial assessment of student learning using work samples, student interviews, and diagnostic assessments. There is little value in teaching content students have already mastered. Yet research shows that valuable classroom time is often spent reteaching known material, especially basic knowledge, while sacrificing time spent on more advanced content (Engel et al., 2016). As with Question 1, a range of challenges can emerge when teams are engaging with this second guiding question. By looking beyond how a barrier presents itself and then exploring its root causes, PLC+ teams can more effectively identify strategies to address or overcome it.

Paving the Way to Activating Question 2: Where are we now?			
Potential Challenges When Activating Question 2	**Possible Reasons**	**Ways to Address and Overcome**	**Discussion Starters and Questions**
The PLC+ is relying on end-of-chapter or end-of-unit assessments to determine current student learning needs—that is, assessment data are rudimentary and generally occur only after teaching.	This can occur when a PLC+ has limited assessment tools at its disposal. It can also happen when the team views students' learning in a somewhat linear manner specific to textbook or other curricular documents.	Introducing evidence from initial assessments is a great way to get the team looking at evidence of student learning early in the investigation cycle. Doing so will help the team focus discussions on learning progressions and how to intervene earlier, as well as on how to be more purposeful in determining how to move learning forward.	"We've been focusing on post-assessment evidence as our primary method to determine where our students are at the end of a teaching cycle. How could we find out much earlier where they are?" "Let's examine where our students are in relation to the learning progressions."
The PLC+ team does not engage in the analysis of student work samples.	This will likely happen if examining student work is not a norm in a PLC+. Also, this can happen if the school has a culture of grading, or if the PLC+ team often scores or grades student work during their meetings instead of analyzing it.	As the activator, providing an opportunity for scoring and analyzing pieces of student work is the starting point. In the beginning, it is important that these work samples are addressing the same content. Model the process so that colleagues can address their apprehension about the process.	"Before we examine our student work, let's review why we used this assignment [these tasks] to determine where students are in their learning." "What sticks out to you in the students' responses? What does it tell us about where they are in relation to the learning progressions? What does it not tell us?"
The PLC+ does not utilize common assessment items; everyone assesses differently.	This occurs in a PLC+ when individual members sit as a group but, once they return to their classrooms, work in "silos."	When assessments differ, PLC+ teams should first identify common skills across content areas to anchor their analysis of student work.	"As we examine the assessment evidence today, let's identify what concepts and skills each one of our assessments addressed in common." "What do we see in the student work in your subject that applies to other subjects?"

(Continued)

(Continued)

Paving the Way to Activating Question 2: Where are we now?			
Potential Challenges When Activating Question 2	**Possible Reasons**	**Ways to Address and Overcome**	**Discussion Starters and Questions**
The PLC+ team members each interpret data differently in their analyses.	Differing perspectives in a PLC+ team can lead to conflicting interpretations of student data, often due to underlying biases about teaching and learning.	All activators will have to address this situation at some point. When this happens, remember not to let it derail the discussion. When disagreements arise, activators should guide the team to view differing perspectives as opportunities—not obstacles—and keep the focus on identifying student needs, not assigning blame.	"We seem to be making different inferences from the data. Why do we think that is the case? *Is it possible we are both right?*" "*Is it possible we are both missing something?*"
The PLC+ members are deflecting critical discussions and blaming each other as to why assessments of student learning look the way they do.	There may be several reasons for this: Teachers may believe students started significantly behind and had too little time to catch up. The assessment may be viewed as unfair, given students' prior knowledge or skill gaps. The results may feel like a reflection on the PLC+ team's effectiveness and teaching ability.	Activators must know how to let individuals share their concerns without allowing the team to move into lamenting or developing a list of barriers that block innovation. Focus on how to respond to the data by using learning progressions that were identified during Question 1: *Where are we going*? This will lead the team to the third guiding question.	"Can we collectively make a commitment to looking at the data with a solution-oriented lens?" "What do we see in the data that we are empowered to influence and impact?" "Does anyone have knowledge of effective strategies to use to support us as we address some of the external challenges we are having?" "Let's focus for now on what the data are actually telling us. What can we learn from this evidence?" "Some of the arguments we are making about these results are valid. However, we have to focus on what we can control: our own actions to advance student learning."

Paving the Way to Activating Question 2: Where are we now?			
Potential Challenges When Activating Question 2	**Possible Reasons**	**Ways to Address and Overcome**	**Discussion Starters and Questions**
Student voices are not a part of the PLC+ initial assessments.	Student evaluations of their own learning are not viewed as critical to understanding where the team is now.	As the activator, develop ways to incorporate student voices into initial assessments.	*"We need to get a full picture of where students are in their learning. We have a great deal of student data, but we need to bring in some specific student-voice evidence as well. What do we think of the examples in Module 7?"* *"All of us agree we need to bring more student voices to the table. What do we want to know? What questions do we feel we need to ask them?"*

Your Additional Challenges and Strategies to Overcome			
Additional Challenges When Activating Question 2	**Possible Reasons for This Challenge**	**Ways You Will Address and Overcome**	**Discussion Starters and Questions**

SUCCESS CHECKLIST

✓	Activation Task
	Note Potential Challenges
☐	Assessment data is rudimentary or occurs post-instruction.
☐	The PLC+ team does not engage in student work sample analysis, does not develop common assessment items across PLC+ members, or offer radically different interpretations of data.
☐	Student voices are not included in initial assessments.
	Activate
☐	Introduce initial common assessments items and incorporate student perspectives early and regularly to inform instruction.
☐	Normalize the practice of analyzing student work in PLC+ meetings.
☐	Encourage discussions that acknowledge multiple perspectives and that involve solutions and actionable steps.
	Reflect and Refine
☐	How much time is spent teaching content that students already know?
☐	Are biases affecting the team's interpretation of student data?
☐	Have you challenged yourself and the team to uncover insights by seeking students' voices about their learning?

Notes

_____
_____
_____
_____
_____
_____
_____
_____
_____
_____
_____
_____
_____

3. ACTIVATING QUESTION 3: HOW DO WE MOVE LEARNING FORWARD?

What strategies can address challenges that arise when activating PLC+ Question 3?						
When						
	Before Meetings	✓	During Meetings		After Meetings	
How Often						
	Planning	✓	Implementation		Reflection	

Strategy in Action | Activating Question 3: How Do We Move Learning Forward?

qrs.ly/1zgpggd

STRATEGY-AT-A-GLANCE

Question 3, "How do we move learning forward?" asks you and your PLC+ colleagues to synthesize the insights from the first two questions and make intentional, evidence-based decisions about how best to advance student learning. Moving learning forward may require team members to engage in ongoing professional learning or to shift their approach to teaching a specific skill or content area. Guiding the team toward meaningful action means being prepared when members default to what's familiar rather than what's necessary—choosing activities over instructional strategies, favoring comfort over impact, or discussing strategies without a clear way to measure their effectiveness.

RECOGNIZING THE NEED

At Morse Middle School, the English language arts PLC+ team of sixth- through eighth-grade teachers has clearly defined their learning goals and success criteria for a unit on argumentative writing. As they begin planning instruction, the team finds themselves flooded with resources—graphic organizers, writing frameworks, digital tools—and are unsure which approaches will truly support student growth. One teacher suggests trying her go-to strategy, while another recommends exploring a new method they recently learned in a workshop. Realizing the need for intentional, evidence-based choices, the team agrees to review student data and research together before selecting the best path to move learning forward.

ACTIVATING WITH THIS STRATEGY

As we have done with the two previous questions, let's explore the challenges and barriers that can hinder the work of a PLC+. Again, please add challenges you anticipate for your unique PLC+ at the base of the tool that follows.

Paving the Way to Activating Question 3: How do we move learning forward?			
Potential Challenges When Activating Question 3	**Possible Reasons**	**Ways to Address and Overcome**	**Discussion Starters and Questions**
Members of the PLC+ team—including the activator—could immediately go to their favorite strategies without considering other possibilities.	Instead of being related to data, a favorite strategy might be reflective of the comfort level of the team and/or the activator. In addition, teams may have limited knowledge of certain effective strategies based on the specific learning needs of the students.	Activators must strive to focus on what actually works best versus personal preferences. It is important that the conversations focus on how to best pair the learning needs of students with specific strategies and actions.	*"Okay, team, let's agree first on what the student learning gap is before we move into strategies. This will help us better ensure that they are aligned. My understanding is that we have identified . . ."* *"Before we go to what we have done in the past, let's brainstorm some new ideas that are focused on what we see in the students' learning gaps."*
PLC+ team members jump directly to activities rather than instructional strategies.	Activity-driven instruction comes from a focus on what the team wants their students to do, thereby overlooking what the team wants their students to learn. In most cases, this jump to activities is unintentional and outside of conscious awareness. This just happens!	**Activators** help PLC+ teams understand that instructional strategies must align with learning intentions and success criteria. These strategies are techniques teachers use to support student progress and promote independent, strategic learning.	*"Those are really engaging activities. I like them. Let's do a quick check to make sure they align with our learning intentions and success criteria."* *"I like what we are thinking about as possible tasks and experiences for the students. First, though, let's determine how we will guide students in their learning before they engage in the tasks."*
PLC+ teams devote a significant amount of time talking about practices and strategies but not about how they will measure the impact.	This can occur when any of the following situations are present: The PLC+ is using (too) many strategies and trying to throw everything possible toward helping students move their learning forward without stopping to consider monitoring that learning. The team has been focused heavily on teaching (not on learning)—so they have been concentrating much more on inputs than on outputs and impact.	There are several ways activators can help guide this discussion so it will have the most impact. The more focused the PLC+ members are on implementing a few solid practices, the better the team will be at executing these with fidelity and quality. For each strategy determined, develop an agreement regarding how often and to what degree it will be implemented in classrooms.	*"We have come up with some great strategies that are aligned to addressing student learning gaps. We need to make sure we have a plan to monitor whether these strategies are moving learning forward."* *"We have agreed on these strategies. Let's make sure we agree on how often they will be implemented. I was thinking three times per week for fifteen minutes. Does that seem like it would be enough?"*

(Continued)

(Continued)

Paving the Way to Activating Question 3: How do we move learning forward?			
Potential Challenges When Activating Question 3	**Possible Reasons**	**Ways to Address and Overcome**	**Discussion Starters and Questions**
		As each strategy is determined and agreed upon, determine how learning will be monitored.	"Now that we have agreed upon the following strategies, let's determine what would show us that they are making an impact. What will we look for in student work and performance, as well as behavior?"
PLC+ team members identify high-impact instructional strategies. However, those strategies do not align with the specific learning gaps identified in the data. In other words, great strategy, wrong time.	When looking at evidence-based instructional strategies, PLC+ teams have a tendency simply to treat these strategies as a checklist, overlooking the alignment of those strategies with the specific learning needs of their students.	The role of the activator is to guide the discussion toward aligning the student learning needs with the best strategies and actions to meet those needs.	"Let's do an alignment check. What are the specific learning gaps we have identified from the data?" "Let's place the strategies right next to these on the whiteboard. Do we see the alignment we know we will need to make sure we are supporting our students?"

Your Additional Challenges and Strategies to Overcome			
Additional Challenges When Activating Question 3	**Possible Reasons for This Challenge**	**Ways You Will Address and Overcome**	**Discussion Starters and Questions**

SUCCESS CHECKLIST

✓	Activation Task
	Note Potential Challenges
☐	Team members default to favorite strategies instead of evidence-based ones.
☐	The PLC+ team jumps directly to assignments and activities, rather than focusing on instructional strategies.
☐	There is an emphasis on strategies without a plan for how to measure their impact.
	Activate
☐	Encourage discussions on aligning strategies with student learning needs before selecting them.
☐	Clarify the difference between engaging activities and instructional strategies; ensure alignment with learning intentions and success criteria.
☐	Develop agreements on strategy implementation frequency and monitoring learning progress.
	Reflect and Refine
☐	Is the team basing the strategy choices on what works best, rather than on what is most comfortable and familiar?
☐	How can the team best measure the effectiveness of the chosen strategies, so that the data can inform continuous improvement of the PLC+ effort?
☐	Has the team regularly reviewed and confirmed that strategies are aligned with the specific learning gaps identified in student data?

Notes

4. ACTIVATING QUESTION 4: WHAT DID WE LEARN TODAY?

	What strategies can address challenges that arise when activating PLC+ Question 4?				
	When				
	Before Meetings	✓	During Meetings		After Meetings
	How Often				
	Planning	✓	Implementation		Reflection

Strategy in Action | Activating Question 4: What Did We Learn Today?

qrs.ly/87gpggf

STRATEGY-AT-A-GLANCE

This question asks PLC+ collaborative teams to examine evidence of learning (aggregated and disaggregated), reflect on what that evidence reveals, and use those insights to guide their next steps. Anticipating barriers—such as uncertainty about which learners are making progress, difficulty reflecting on learning, a tendency to focus on external rather than internal factors, or a lack of awareness around professional learning needs—help activators keep the work focused and maintain forward momentum.

RECOGNIZING THE NEED

At Oak Hill Elementary, the fourth-grade PLC+ team gathers after school to review exit tickets from their math lesson on multidigit multiplication. Ms. Carter notices that most students grasped the algorithm, but Mr. Lee points out that several multilingual learners struggled with word problems despite solving the equations correctly. The team realizes they need to adjust their instruction to include more language supports and visual aids during problem-solving activities. This reflection sharpens their focus on who benefited from the day's lesson and who needs additional support, guiding their next steps with clarity and purpose.

ACTIVATING WITH THIS STRATEGY

Successfully addressing this question will leave the PLC+ laser focused on who did and did not benefit from instruction—the topic of guiding Question 5. This section explores the challenges and barriers that can hinder the work of a PLC+ when teams ask about what they have learned. As you read this section, you may become aware of challenges you believe your unique PLC+ might encounter. If so, add them to the list.

Paving the Way to Activating Question 4: What did we learn today?

Potential Challenges When Activating Question 4	Possible Reasons	Ways to Address and Overcome	Discussion Starters and Questions
The PLC+ team—including the activator—are not clear on which learners are or are not making progress.	The primary reason for this challenge is that the team has not devoted time to determining what progress looks like for specific learning outcomes.	Of course, determining progress will come from examining assessment evidence. Determining what to look for before collecting assessment evidence as well as during the analysis of student work can support activators in moving their PLC+ forward.	"I have work samples from last year. Let's analyze these alongside our standards to develop a list of look-fors." "For this unit, what would we like our learners to be able to do at the end of each day?"
Some PLC+ teams are not used to reflecting on their learning. This often leads to moments of uncomfortable silence or avoidance of reflective practices.	This barrier appears in a PLC+ for several reasons. In some cases, team members do not want to look as if they are not good at their jobs. Another possibility is that the PLC+ team, school, or district has no culture of reflection.	Activators can move their PLC+ out of this type of stagnation by making sure specific routines and protocols are followed for reflection. In addition, team cohesion and the establishment of credibility, efficacy, and collaboration are essential in providing a safe environment for reflection.	"Okay, those are some good takeaways from what we learned today. Let's try to break some of them down a little more . . ." "I like what you said there. We have to go past just acknowledging that there are gaps in student learning and focus on specific levels of the learning progressions. What, specifically, are those gaps? Who else has a thought on that?"
The PLC+ focuses on external factors outside the control of teachers when responding to what was learned (or not) today.	In this situation, PLC+ team members may feel that the assessment in and of itself was not fair to the students based on each learner's level of readiness. In addition, team members may get defensive because they interpret the results as a direct reflection on their identity as an effective teacher.	When this happens, a good activator knows how to take a shared comment and transform it into a reflection without it becoming an attack on the person doing the sharing. At the same time, activators must make sure the PLC+ focuses on what members have control of in the classroom. Operating and process norms will help with this situation.	"Let's talk about what we have learned here today, particularly about the strategies we are using . . ." "Let's debrief Question 4: What did we learn today? Let's go around the table once and each share a reflection." "Those are all relevant points, but I believe we all agree that our colleagues in the previous grade level are working hard as well. Let's focus back on what we learned about our impact."

(Continued)

(Continued)

Paving the Way to Activating Question 4: What did we learn today?			
Potential Challenges When Activating Question 4	**Possible Reasons**	**Ways to Address and Overcome**	**Discussion Starters and Questions**
PLC+ teams might recognize the learning needs of their students but not the professional learning needs of their own members.	It can be difficult for professionals to admit their own learning needs. This difficulty comes from a fear of looking incompetent, being afraid of showing vulnerability, or simply not knowing what they don't know.	This type of reflective practice is important for the activators to recognize. There is a tight connection between Questions 3 and 4: "How do we move learning forward?" and "What did we learn today?" How is the team examining the impact of the strategies selected to move learning forward? This examination determines what the team is currently learning in its PLC+ journey, as well as what members might *need to learn* as professionals to move student learning forward.	"We have been able to agree that, according to the evidence, our students as a whole have some specific learning gaps in ____. What do we need to learn ourselves to help best support them moving forward?" "We have really done a great job diagnosing what the learning gaps are for multiple groups of students. Now we need to talk about what this means for us as a PLC+ team moving forward. Could you get us started by offering your thoughts?"

Your Additional Challenges and Strategies to Overcome			
Additional Challenges When Activating Question 4	**Possible Reasons for This Challenge**	**Ways You Will Address and Overcome**	**Discussion Starters and Questions**

SUCCESS CHECKLIST

✓	Activation Task
	Note Potential Challenges
☐	There is a lack of clarity on which learners are making progress.
☐	The PLC+ team is unfamiliar with reflective practices and tends to focus on external factors rather than on actionable insights.
☐	There is a failure to recognize professional learning needs within the PLC+ team.
	Activate
☐	Define clear indicators of progress and analyze assessment evidence before and after student work evaluations.
☐	Establish structured reflection routines and protocols to create a climate of safety and trust within PLC+ teams.
☐	Examine the impact of instructional strategies and determine the professional learning needs required for improvement.
	Reflect and Refine
☐	What does progress look like for specific learning outcomes? How can the team measure it effectively?
☐	Why is reflective practice uncomfortable? How can the team build a culture of open, nonjudgmental reflection?
☐	How can the team shift the conversation from external factors to aspects of teaching and learning in their control?

Notes

5. ACTIVATING QUESTION 5: WHO BENEFITED AND WHO DID NOT BENEFIT?

What strategies can address challenges that arise when activating PLC+ Question 5?					
When					
	Before Meetings	✓	During Meetings		After Meetings
How Often					
	Planning	✓	Implementation		Reflection

Strategy in Action | Activating Question 5: Who benefited and who did not benefit?

qrs.ly/21gpggg

STRATEGY-AT-A-GLANCE

To answer the question of benefit truthfully and accurately, teams must return to the learning intentions, success criteria, and learning progressions that define what benefit looks like. Be prepared to respond when you recognize that your focus has become too narrow, your expectations are too low, or your strategies are falling short of producing deep and transferable learning for students.

RECOGNIZING THE NEED

During a PLC+ meeting at Riverbend Middle School, the seventh-grade science team reviews assessment data from their unit on ecosystems.

"Most of my students did really well," says Mr. Alvarez, "but when I disaggregated the data, I noticed that several of my learners who didn't score highly on the initial assessment didn't meet the unit success criteria."

Ms. Langley nods and adds, "I saw the same pattern—our high-performing students soared, but we didn't provide enough scaffolding for those who needed language or reading support."

The team agrees to adjust their instructional approach to ensure that all students, especially those who didn't benefit, receive the same quality of learning experiences moving forward.

ACTIVATING WITH THIS STRATEGY

What makes this question essential to the PLC+ framework is also what makes it challenging—and at times, uncomfortable. PLC+ teams must face the evidence that reveals which learners did not benefit from the instruction provided, and they must investigate the potential patterns or commonalities among those learners. Take time

34 · 50 Strategies for Activating Your PLC+

to explore the challenges and barriers that may hinder your team's ability to reflect honestly on what educators and students have learned. Space is provided for you to note any unique challenges you anticipate that your own PLC+ team might face.

Paving the Way to Activating Question 5: Who benefited and who did not benefit?			
Potential Challenges When Activating Question 5	**Possible Reasons**	**Ways to Address and Overcome**	**Discussion Starters and Questions**
The PLC+ team—including you—find that the instructional strategies the team has focused on are addressing only one group (e.g., children in poverty or children with a disability).	This could happen for two very plausible but different reasons: The PLC+ team hasn't engaged in analysis of or dialogue about multiple groups of students. The PLC+ has some issues with, fear of, or resistance to examining the learning and achievement of multiple groups of students.	One way to prepare for addressing this issue is to ensure that data are disaggregated by various identifiable characteristics, such as gender, race, socioeconomic status (SES), mobility, Individualized Education Program (IEP)/504, or language acquisition status. Make this review of the data part of the agenda for any data review meeting—that is, ask, "Do we see any discrepancies in achievement or progress relative to students' demographic or other characteristics?"	"How does this strategy impact the various students we serve? (e.g., were there differences in achievement and/or progress related to gender, race, SES, mobility, IEP/504, or other student characteristics?)" "Do we see any discrepancies in achievement or progress relative to student characteristics? If so, what are they?"
The PLC+ holds low expectations.	There is evidence that teachers hold different expectations for students of different racial, ethnic, and socioeconomic backgrounds. Findings also support the idea that if teachers have high expectations, they tend to have these for all their students. When readiness levels vary, teachers need to find ways to provide pathways for learning for all their students without diluting the rigorous standards to which students need to be held accountable.	Analyzing standards can be a great way to ensure that teams are appropriately looking at the rigor level that lies within each standard. As the activator, your role is to ensure that your PLC+ has a clear understanding that the level of rigor within the standard is key.	"Did the tasks that we engaged students in match appropriately the skills and concepts in our standards?" "Did the tasks that we engaged students in match the rigor in our standards?" "Are we scoring student work in alignment with the skills, concepts, and rigor levels in the standards?"

(Continued)

(Continued)

Paving the Way to Activating Question 5: Who benefited and who did not benefit?			
Potential Challenges When Activating Question 5	**Possible Reasons**	**Ways to Address and Overcome**	**Discussion Starters and Questions**
The strategies and tasks shared during PLC+ are primarily at surface-level knowledge acquisition and do not induce student learning at deep and transferable levels.	Deep learning requires intentional planning by PLC+ teams. Because most classroom activities remain at the surface level, superficial learning is common. When data reveal performance gaps among student groups, a team's collective efficacy is tested—calling for proactive solutions, not blame.	This is where the "plus" in PLC+ comes to life. Teams can explore the differences between surface, deep, and transfer learning, then begin connecting content to instructional tasks that support all three. Analyzing standards can also clarify when deeper learning experiences are needed and how to design instruction that meets that level of rigor.	"Which standards support opportunities for deep or transfer learning experiences?" "What surface-level knowledge do students need to have to ensure that they are able to engage in deeper learning experiences?" "What phase or phases of learning are our learning tasks linked to?"

Your Additional Challenges and Strategies to Overcome			
Additional Challenges When Activating Question 5	**Possible Reasons for This Challenge**	**Ways You Will Address and Overcome**	**Discussion Starters and Questions**

SUCCESS CHECKLIST

✓	Activation Task
	Note Potential Challenges
☐	Some student groups are not benefiting from instruction at the same rate as others.
☐	There is resistance or discomfort in examining achievement among different student groups.
☐	There are low expectations for certain groups of learners or superficial learning activities that do not lead to deep or transferable learning.
	Activate
☐	Disaggregate data by gender, race, SES, mobility, IEP/504, attendance, or language status to identify discrepancies in achievement, and facilitate open dialogue about benefit.
☐	Analyze standards rigorously to ensure learning pathways are designed for all students without lowering expectations.
☐	Plan and implement tasks that move students from surface-level knowledge to deeper learning and application.
	Reflect and Refine
☐	Are there patterns in student achievement gaps? What factors might contribute to them?
☐	How can the team create a PLC+ climate where all students' learning outcomes are examined?
☐	How well do the team's instructional tasks align with the depth of learning required by the standards?

Notes

ACTIVATOR SKILLS AND ABILITIES

An Introduction to Activator Skills and Abilities

qrs.ly/aogpggi

6. ACTIVATOR SKILLS AND ABILITIES: ACTIVATING TO ACHIEVE A TRUE IMPACT ON LEARNING

How do we get past disagreements and focus on solutions that will measurably impact learning?					
When					
	Before Meetings	✓	During Meetings		After Meetings
How Often					
	Planning	✓	Implementation		Reflection

Strategy in Action | Activating to Achieve a True Impact on Learning

qrs.ly/czgpggk

STRATEGY-AT-A-GLANCE

Teams can get mired in what is convenient or familiar, rather than in what is informed by evidence and research. Use this strategy when you notice that the team is having difficulty innovating or is drawing on instructional strategies that have proven to be ineffective, such as focusing on learning styles or engaging in round robin reading. It is also useful to refocus the team's attention on the need to support their own professional learning to examine evidence-based practices.

RECOGNIZING THE NEED

As the PLC+ teams at Harriet Tubman Elementary School focus on writing strategies, several suggestions about how to move learning forward involve approaches that are not associated with a high impact on student learning. One of the members of the PLC+, who recognizes these potential missteps, puts it this way: "The ideas we generated are things I have heard do not work in writing instruction. That is why we are already not doing those very things." How does an activator turn disagreement and disbelief into something that has a true impact on learning?

ACTIVATING WITH THIS STRATEGY

Often this type of PLC+ work barrier stems from not knowing. And yet, when left unchecked, the barrier impacts the PLC+ effort and student learning. In fact, we could easily reframe this barrier and label it as "not knowing what works best." On the other hand, some teachers may be well aware of what works best, but they might not know how to match the right approach with the right content, student, and time. Here are three ways to help the team realize the true impact on learning you seek—beginning with leveraging data.

Approach	How to Activate
Start (and end) with data.	To ensure that teams maximize impact on student learning, use collected data to inform decisions. Team members engage in dialogue about what the data say must be accomplished.
Let urgency influence your approach.	There are many different approaches and strategies that can result in a high impact on student learning. Part of the PLC+ team's work is making strategic, shared decisions about what to implement when. If the PLC+ dialogue shifts toward approaches that will result in minimal learning, guide the conversation toward the things that are the most urgently related to student progress. This will increase the odds of picking a high-yield approach.
Pursue professional learning as a solution.	Have you ever thought of professional learning as approaches to overcoming barriers? PLC+ teams can benefit from professional learning on evidence-based practices and what works best when, which they can then apply to their unique context and related needs. As a result, they increase the chance of predictable results—for the PLC+ and the students they teach.

SUCCESS CHECKLIST

✓	Activation Task
	Note Potential Challenges
☐	Teams are selecting strategies without using data.
☐	Teams are making decisions based on familiarity rather than on impact.
☐	There is no—or limited—use of professional learning as a tool.
	Activate
☐	Use data at the start and end of every PLC+ meeting.
☐	Guide conversations toward high-impact strategies.
☐	Engage in targeted, intentional professional learning to refine strategies.
	Reflect and Refine
☐	Is the team making data-driven decisions?
☐	Is urgency influencing the team's work? How can the team best use urgency and then reflect their findings in the PLC+ effort?
☐	How effectively is the team applying professional learning?

7. ACTIVATOR SKILLS AND ABILITIES: ASSESSING YOUR ACTIVATOR FITNESS LEVEL

How ready am I to fulfill the role of activator in my PLC+?					
When					
✓	Before Meetings		During Meetings		After Meetings
How Often					
✓	Planning		Implementation		Reflection

Strategy in Action | Assessing Your Activator Fitness Level

qrs.ly/6hgpggl

STRATEGY-AT-A-GLANCE

Use *the 5Cs—clarity, consciousness, competence, confidence, and credibility*—to assess your own readiness for leadership in the PLC+ activator role. With your gained understanding, identify priority opportunities to expand and extend your activator skills.

RECOGNIZING THE NEED

Mary Beth Rogers was among the excited participants who volunteered for her school's first PLC+ effort. Seeing it as a true opportunity to positively impact learning for her students, she eagerly accepted the call. Recognizing Mary Beth's interest, her principal encouraged her involvement and challenged her to take an active leadership role in the PLC+ implementation. Initially, Mary Beth was "all in," even though she hadn't really led anything like this before. In time, however, as she tried her best to activate the work, she realized her own skillset might be influencing the limited impact she was initially experiencing as an activator.

ACTIVATING WITH THIS STRATEGY

This book is designed to provide strategies for activators to use at each stage of the PLC+ journey. We are reminded of an often-heard analogy: "Put your face mask on first, before helping others." This strategy involves helping yourself to assist the team. Have you taken time to self-assess your own skills and capabilities against skills used by successful activators?

Garmston and Wellman (2016) identified specific qualities necessary for effective team collaboration, which they refer to as *the 5Cs: clarity, consciousness, competence, confidence, and credibility*. The 5Cs have much to contribute to your success as a PLC+ activator. As you consider each element, consider your skills, and list some ideas for yourself as an *activator* in your PLC+.

Activator Quality	Description	Examples	My Current Skill Level
Clarity	Uses precise language to minimize ambiguity and limit unnecessary frustration.	"Let's focus on a key challenge we all face—building student confidence in chemistry with limiting reactants. Jenna, what's one approach that's worked well in your classroom?" "Based on the standard, students need to understand how to add and subtract fractions with unlike denominators and apply those skills to solve problems."	
Consciousness	Remains aware of signals being conveyed through body language, voice inflection, and restlessness.	"It looks like we're starting to fade a bit—let's take a five-minute stretch break to recharge before we dive into the second half." "Robert, it seems like you might see this differently. Would you be open to sharing your perspective?"	
Competence	Demonstrates skill in the craft of activation by using the right type of conversation at the right moment—knowing when to guide assertively and when to step back and invite reflection.	"I'm hearing lots of energy and great ideas flying around—which is a good problem to have! Let's channel that momentum into two smaller groups so we can dig in more deeply. One group can focus on strategies that support struggling learners, and the other can focus on ways to extend learning for students who are ready for more. Take about ten minutes, and then we'll regroup to share what you come up with."	
Confidence	Demonstrates strong self-efficacy and confidence in their ability to help the team achieve goals and navigate challenges together.	"We've all seen what works in different ways, and I think we can really build on that together. I tried something new last week that showed some promise—would you be open to helping me think through how it might be refined or adapted?"	
Credibility	Builds and sustains trust over time by being honest, impartial, fair, and willing to own mistakes.	"Last week gave me a few moments that really stretched my thinking. I'd love to walk through a couple of them and hear your thoughts on what I might do differently next time." "Let's each take a moment to name one challenge we faced recently and what it taught us. It's a good way to surface lessons we might otherwise keep to ourselves."	

Source: Adapted from Garmston, R. J., & Wellman, B. M. (2016). *The adaptive school: A sourcebook for developing collaborative groups* (3rd ed.). Rowman & Littlefield.

SUCCESS CHECKLIST

✓	Activation Task
	Note Potential Challenges
☐	There are personal skill gaps in leadership and activation.
☐	The PLC+ team dynamics and engagement levels are weak.
☐	Confidence or credibility is frequently lacking.
	Activate
☐	Self-assess skills using the 5Cs framework.
☐	Seek mentorship or coaching from experienced activators.
☐	Actively practice clear and precise communication strategies.
	Reflect and Refine
☐	How effectively are you using the 5Cs in your leadership?
☐	In what areas do you need to grow to be a more competent activator?
☐	How do your actions influence the engagement and success of the team?

Notes

_____
_____
_____
_____
_____
_____
_____
_____
_____
_____
_____
_____
_____
_____
_____

8. ACTIVATOR SKILLS AND ABILITIES: DEFINING YOUR ACTIVATOR ROLE

What does being an activator, and leading the activation of a PLC+ team, mean to you?					
When					
✓	Before Meetings		During Meetings		After Meetings
How Often					
✓	Planning		Implementation		Reflection

STRATEGY-AT-A-GLANCE

As you assume, or continue, the work in the activator role, it is important that you have a true and deep understanding of the terms *activator* and *activation*. When you dedicate time to exploring each term, you will find diverse definitions and uses of the words. This strategy helps you come to clarity about what each term means to help you carry out the critical role of activator in the PLC+.

RECOGNIZING THE NEED

As the PLC+ meeting got underway, Ms. Rivera asked, "So, who's actually leading this conversation today?"

Mr. Allen replied, "I think we need to talk about the activator role. I've heard it described as someone who keeps the group focused on student learning and drives the work forward."

Mrs. Jenkins nodded and said, "Right now, we're just sharing ideas without a clear direction—an activator could help us stay on track and push us deeper."

The team agreed that defining and selecting an activator was essential to making their PLC+ time more purposeful and impactful.

ACTIVATING WITH THIS STRATEGY

Look up the word *activator* and jot down the definitions of that word. When we did this ourselves, we found multiple definitions. We particularly enjoyed learning that there is an "activator" device used by chiropractors when the goal is to produce enough force to move the vertebrae toward alignment, but not so much force as to cause injury. Consider that analogy within the context of leading change. Defining your role as an *activator* on a team means stepping into a space where you're committed to moving ideas into action, energizing others, and driving momentum—all without pushing *too* far.

Defining the Role	Evidence
Reflect on personal strengths and values.	Do I naturally take initiative? Do I thrive on getting things started? Activators often realize their role through self-awareness. If you're the one who says, *"Let's try it,"* or *"How do we move this forward?"*—then you're already acting as an activator.
Identify gaps in team dynamics.	Teams often have thinkers, planners, and evaluators—but fewer people who push things into motion. Activators notice when ideas stall and feel compelled to catalyze the next steps.
Pay attention to what energizes you.	If you're most energized when taking action, starting projects, or creating pilot versions of ideas, you're operating in activator mode. You might notice that you love momentum more than perfection—another clue.
Get feedback from colleagues.	Others may already see you as the spark plug or momentum builder. Feedback like *"You always get us going"* or *"You helped me take action"* affirms the activator identity.
Learn from models of activation.	Study how others act as activators—team leads, coaches, or even people in different industries. Borrow language, strategies, and stances that feel authentic to you.
Develop a personal activator mission statement.	Create a statement like this one: *"I help ideas take flight by initiating action, motivating others, and removing barriers to progress."* This will then become your compass for knowing when and how to act.

SUCCESS CHECKLIST

✓	Activation Task
	Note Potential Challenges
☐	The activator has not considered the broad and varied definitions of the words *activate* and *activator*.
☐	The activator is not in touch with what energizes them.
☐	The activator does not seek out and listen to the feedback and insights of colleagues and other activators.
	Activate
☐	Come to your own personal definitions for the terms *activate* and *activator*.
☐	Share your definitions, understandings, and examples with your PLC+ team, and invite conversation to come to team clarity about the role.
☐	Revisit your notes right before you step into the regularly scheduled PLC+ meeting to recall your personal reasons for taking on the activator role and the parts of the role that mean the most to you. Then manifest them in your leadership of the meeting.
	Reflect and Refine
☐	How do your initial descriptors for the activator role change at the conclusion of the first, and each subsequent, PLC+ cycle?
☐	How can you share your reflections and realizations with the team to help all participants better understand the contributions of an activator?
☐	When the PLC+ effort realizes success, have you taken time to more deeply understand—and document—the team's impact and your activator contributions that have added to that success?

Notes

_____
_____
_____
_____
_____
_____
_____
_____
_____
_____
_____

9. ACTIVATOR SKILLS AND ABILITIES: DEVELOPING SUCCESSFUL PLC+ ACTIVATORS

How do I cultivate the mindset and behaviors of an effective PLC+ activator to build trust, challenge thinking, and support growth?					
When					
✓	Before Meetings		During Meetings		After Meetings
How Often					
✓	Planning		Implementation		Reflection

Strategy in Action | Developing Successful PLC+ Activators

qrs.ly/lbgpggm

STRATEGY-AT-A-GLANCE

Activators are essential to the success of PLC+ teams, serving as catalysts who model learning, challenge thinking, and build trust. This strategy is grounded in five key characteristics of effective activators. The five characteristics—credibility, a commitment to adult learning, the ability to challenge constructively, a belief in universal growth, and resilience—are not innate; they can be developed over time. By cultivating these qualities intentionally, educators can strengthen team dynamics and drive deeper learning for students and teachers.

RECOGNIZING THE NEED

At Heritage High School, the PLC+ for ninth-grade teachers is running out of steam. Mr. Lewis, the history teacher, voices concern that no one is really pushing the team's thinking forward. Ms. Tate, a new science teacher, admits she isn't sure how to contribute meaningfully in the absence of clear leadership. When Ms. Hart, the instructional coach, asks, "What if we identify an activator for our team?" the group looks up, intrigued—realizing they need someone to guide, challenge, and unify their work.

ACTIVATING WITH THIS STRATEGY

Effective PLC+ activators model behaviors that build credibility, spark learning, and promote resilience. To step fully into the role of an activator, educators must first engage in self-reflection to identify their current strengths and areas for growth across these five characteristics. For example, building *credibility* may require consistently following through on commitments or deepening instructional expertise. Strengthening *a commitment to adult learning* could involve seeking out professional development opportunities or facilitating team-based inquiry.

50 Strategies for Activating Your PLC+

Constructively challenging colleagues means learning to ask probing questions that promote reflection without causing defensiveness. A *belief in universal growth* challenges educators to hold high expectations for all learners—including their peers—whereas *resilience* calls for navigating setbacks with persistence and optimism. As educators develop these traits, they not only enhance their individual effectiveness but also model the very learning culture they seek to cultivate within the PLC+ framework. The following table outlines how activators can translate each trait into specific actions that support continuous improvement on a PLC+ team.

Activator Quality	Description
High Credibility	Build trust by being consistent, prepared, and open to feedback. Develop strong relationships with colleagues and students by following through on commitments and demonstrating instructional competence.
Lead Adult Learning	Facilitate collaborative learning experiences and coach peers by modeling curiosity and a willingness to reflect. Activate others' thinking by asking thought-provoking questions and sharing strategies transparently.
Challenge Effectively	Create a culture where ideas can be respectfully questioned. Offer and invite constructive feedback, and model how to push thinking without judgment.
Belief in Growth for All	Operate from the belief that every teacher and student can improve. Show this through high expectations, inclusive language, and a celebration of growth wherever it occurs.
Demonstrate Resilience	Stay grounded in moments of tension or adversity. Normalize challenges as part of the improvement process and model perseverance and recovery in the face of setbacks.

SUCCESS CHECKLIST

✓	Activation Task
	Note Potential Challenges
☐	PLC+ team members are hesitant or lack confidence when presenting ideas or giving feedback.
☐	There is an overreliance on one or two voices in the PLC+, without distributed leadership.
☐	There are signs of disengagement or resistance during reflection or discussion.
	Activate
☐	Identify potential activators and offer support through coaching, modeling, or targeted professional learning.
☐	Note the benefits to the entire team of increased credibility, a commitment to adult learning, the ability to challenge constructively, a belief in universal growth, and resilience.
☐	Celebrate resilience by acknowledging small wins and modeling how to bounce back from setbacks.
	Reflect and Refine
☐	How do you model credibility, resilience, and growth in your work with others?
☐	What do you do to help your team reflect critically and move forward together?
☐	In what ways are you helping others lead, learn, and persevere within the PLC+ environment?

Notes

_____
_____
_____
_____
_____
_____
_____
_____
_____
_____
_____
_____

10. ACTIVATOR SKILLS AND ABILITIES: FACILITATION SELF-ASSESSMENT

How do I strengthen my facilitation skills to ensure that my PLC+ team stays focused, engaged, and purpose driven?					
When					
✓	Before Meetings		During Meetings		After Meetings
How Often					
✓	Planning		Implementation		Reflection

STRATEGY-AT-A-GLANCE

Although we acknowledge that the role of activator is more than facilitation, facilitation remains a significant skill that activators regularly contribute to the benefit of their PLC+ team. This self-assessment will help you review and consider a range of facilitation skills. Use it to identify your strengths and opportunities for growth.

RECOGNIZING THE NEED

As the PLC+ meeting drags into its second hour, Mr. Chen sighs and asks, "Wait—what exactly are we supposed to be doing with this data again?"

Ms. Morales, who had led the session without clearly stating goals, looks around and admits, "Honestly, I was hoping we'd just figure it out together."

Meanwhile, two team members haven't spoken at all, and one has already packed up her things. Watching the dynamic unfold, Ms. Ruiz realizes this isn't a content problem—it is a facilitation issue.

ACTIVATING WITH THIS STRATEGY

Facilitation is the intentional process of guiding a team's conversations, decisions, and collaborative work to ensure that all voices are heard, goals remain clear, and progress is made efficiently and equitably. Unlike direction or management, facilitation focuses on creating the conditions for collective thinking, problem solving, and shared ownership. Effective facilitation helps teams stay focused, navigate conflict productively, and build psychological safety, which is essential for honest dialogue and innovation. In collaborative settings like PLC+ teams, strong facilitation ensures that meetings are not only well structured but also deeply reflective and action oriented—maximizing the impact of professional learning on student outcomes.

Use the following Self-Assessment Tool to review and rate your current level of facilitation skills. Based on the ratings, note your strengths as well as areas of opportunity. Remember: Often the best way to develop new skills—or enhance existing ones—is to build upon an established strength.

Skill	Beginning		Developing	Modeling	
I am able to open a learning space or meeting effectively, and I am able to establish a positive climate right from the beginning.	1	2	3	4	5
I can communicate purposes (why), desired outcomes (what), and instructions (how) clearly and confidently to the group.	1	2	3	4	5
I am aware of the different facilitation style needs of groups, and I am able to adapt my style to suit the occasion.	1	2	3	4	5
I use active listening effectively (e.g., summarizing and reflecting back what's being said accurately and objectively).	1	2	3	4	5
I am able to intentionally use nonverbal communication moves.	1	2	3	4	5
I am able to draw out quieter members of the group.	1	2	3	4	5
I am able to use a range of questions to promote open and honest discussion that will surface multiple perspectives.	1	2	3	4	5
I am able to use a range of questions to promote critical self-reflection and self-directed learning.	1	2	3	4	5
I am able to manage situations where there is emotional processing and release.	1	2	3	4	5
I am conscious of the dynamics of how race, class, gender, and power impact participants in the group.	1	2	3	4	5
I am able to encourage honest communication and facilitate productive dialogue on issues of equity (e.g., race, gender, expectations, beliefs, disproportionate outcomes, etc.).	1	2	3	4	5
I can facilitate conflict between members of the group effectively.	1	2	3	4	5

(Continued)

(Continued)

Skill	Beginning		Developing		Modeling
I can productively respond to disruptive or overtalkative members of the group.	1	2	3	4	5
I can give respectful, specific, and actionable feedback to individuals and the group.	1	2	3	4	5
I can close a learning space that allows for a synthesis of learning and appreciation for the collective.	1	2	3	4	5

Source: Tool developed by the National Equity Project

SUCCESS CHECKLIST

✓	Activation Task
	Note Potential Challenges
☐	PLC+ group discussions lack structure, focus, or inclusive participation.
☐	There are patterns of disengagement or dominance from specific individuals during PLC+ meetings.
☐	The team struggles to navigate emotionally charged topics or equity-related dialogue.
	Activate
☐	Use the Self-Assessment Tool to evaluate your facilitation skills across key areas.
☐	Identify one or two specific facilitation practices to improve or strengthen.
☐	Model empathy, clarity, and adaptability during meetings, especially in times of tension or disagreement.
	Reflect and Refine
☐	Which facilitation strengths are you consistently modeling for the PLC+ team?
☐	Where do you feel least confident in your facilitation practice, and why?
☐	How do your actions as an activator promote equity, inclusion, and collaborative growth?

11. ACTIVATOR SKILLS AND ABILITIES: FACILITATING WITH GRACE

How can I apply the quality of grace when facilitating in my activator role?					
When					
	Before Meetings	✓	During Meetings		After Meetings
How Often					
	Planning	✓	Implementation		Reflection

STRATEGY-AT-A-GLANCE

Think of a person in your life who moves through the world with grace. Not necessarily a physical grace, but a form that lightens your burden and touches you at your core. Successful activators can help their PLC+ teams through the application of grace, including elements of empathy, respect, and distress-free authority.

RECOGNIZING THE NEED

The moment Ms. Holloway closes her notebook and mutters, "I'm done trying to justify my teaching," the remaining members of the PLC+ seem to freeze. Mr. Elkins shifts uncomfortably but says nothing, while others look to their activator, Ms. Hernandez, whose calm presence seems to settle the tension before it unravels.

"Let's take a breath," she says softly, "and make space for frustration without losing sight of the respect we owe each other."

With quiet empathy and the steady presence of graceful leadership, Ms. Hernandez guides the group back into conversation—not to solve everything, but to simply remind the teachers that they are still a team.

ACTIVATING WITH THIS STRATEGY

Author John Heron (1999) articulates what he calls "Keys of Grace" to describe the qualities of a helping professional. Heron believes that inner grace is a spiritual endowment that everyone can cultivate. His three "keys" of grace—*empathy, respect for people,* and *distress-free authority*—may sound basic, but they can be extraordinarily difficult to enact when people's fear and anxiety are in play. As Sylwester (1994) told us, "Our emotional system is a complex, widely-distributed, and error-prone system that defines our basic personality early in life, and is quite resistant to change," and noted that "emotion is often a more powerful determinant of our behavior than our brain's logical/rational processes" (p. 60).

If you can communicate warmth, acceptance, absolute respect, and distress-free authority as the activator of a PLC+ team, you exponentially increase your chances of facilitating a positive group dynamic. The three main qualities of grace to pay close attention to during facilitation are presented in the following table.

Key	Description
Empathy	I consistently demonstrate warm concern, active listening, and genuine acceptance for each member of the group, creating a space where individuals feel seen and valued.
Respect for People	I honor the full autonomy of each team member, recognizing their agency in choosing when and how to learn and grow, without imposing my own timeline or expectations.
Distress-Free Authority	I maintain self-awareness and emotional regulation during facilitation, ensuring that my own stress or anxiety does not influence my actions or disrupt the group's progress.

Source: Tool developed by the National Equity Project

SUCCESS CHECKLIST

✓	Activation Task
	Note Potential Challenges
☐	Emotional withdrawal, defensiveness, or frustration disrupts PLC+ team cohesion.
☐	Team members feel unheard, disrespected, or invalidated.
☐	The activator reacts from personal stress rather than leads with calm clarity.
	Activate
☐	Respond to tension with empathy and acknowledgment rather than immediate problem solving.
☐	Hold space for emotional expression while gently reinforcing shared values of respect and collaboration.
☐	Cultivate internal awareness to model distress-free authority.
	Reflect and Refine
☐	How do you respond when emotions run high in the PLC+ team?
☐	Are you offering grace in the form of empathy, respect, and distress-free authority—even in difficult moments?
☐	How can you build your capacity to stay grounded and lead with clarity when others feel overwhelmed?

12. ACTIVATOR SKILLS AND ABILITIES: FINDING THE KEY ACTIVATOR

Once we know the kind of activator we need, how do we go about finding the right person?					
When					
✓	Before Meetings		During Meetings		After Meetings
How Often					
✓	Planning		Implementation		Reflection

STRATEGY-AT-A-GLANCE

Although you may know the skills you're looking for in an activator, finding the right team member or members to fulfill the role can be a challenge. Giving full consideration to potential activators, having clear expectations for the role, and proactively planning and managing time investments contribute to successful performance in the role.

RECOGNIZING THE NEED

April Davidson, a middle school science teacher, offers the following reflection on her PLC+ team's engagement in facilitation: "Whenever it came time to decide who would guide our data conversation, everyone suddenly became very interested in their laptops. No one would make eye contact, and the room would go quiet."

She explains that before the PLC+ routines were well established, team members often assumed someone else would naturally take the reins. She says, "I have to admit, even I would sometimes hope someone else would speak up first."

Ms. Davidson notes that occasionally, after a long pause, a team member would reluctantly agree to lead just to end the silence. But that sense of obligation rather than ownership ended up stalling the team's momentum. She adds, "It felt like we were dragging ourselves through the work instead of stepping into it with purpose. And that showed in our outcomes."

Ms. Davidson shares how she and her colleagues were finally able to move forward. "We had several coaching conversations with a school-based instructional lead, which allowed us to create a shared facilitation plan that distributed leadership across the cycle." She says, "It gave us clarity and confidence. It didn't feel like a burden anymore—it felt like something we built together."

ACTIVATING WITH THIS STRATEGY

Likely, the key activator is sitting among you. Remember, all members of the PLC+ team can be activators. But when we are talking about the person charged with driving things forward, it is important to get a bit more specific in terms of placing the right person in this critical role.

Here are three strategies for consideration, each of which supports the person-activator match.

Approach	How to Activate
Observe behaviors.	Notice who naturally moves conversations from discussion to decision making. Look for team members who often say things like, *"What's our next step?"* or *"Let's try it."* Identify who brings energy and momentum to meetings without dominating the space.
Use team input.	Ask the team, *"Who helps us move forward when we feel stuck?"* or *"Who helps turn ideas into action?"* Nominate peers based on past actions rather than titles or roles.
Review past cycles.	Look back at successful PLC+ cycles. Who facilitated the work well? Who ensured that the team stayed focused and followed through?
Try rotating the role.	Let everyone try being the activator for a short cycle. Reflect afterward as a team: Who thrived? Who felt most aligned with the role?
Reduce other commitments as a team.	People designated as activators need assistance from the team in managing responsibilities. Work as a team to identify competing demands on the activator, and collectively redistribute responsibility.

SUCCESS CHECKLIST

✓	Activation Task
	Note Potential Challenges
☐	There are awkward silences when selecting an activator.
☐	The team expectations are not clearly defined.
☐	Outside commitments are interfering with the activator's focus.
	Activate
☐	Solicit help from trusted colleagues to step up as an activator.
☐	Clearly define and come to agreement on expectations for all PLC+ roles.
☐	Reduce outside commitments to allow focus on PLC+ work.
	Reflect and Refine
☐	How does reluctance to lead negatively impact team effectiveness?
☐	Are expectations for roles and responsibilities clearly communicated?
☐	How does reducing outside commitments benefit the activator's performance?

Notes

_____
_____
_____
_____
_____
_____
_____
_____
_____
_____
_____
_____
_____
_____

CONTINUOUS IMPROVEMENT

An Introduction to Continuous Improvement

qrs.ly/wogpggo

13. CONTINUOUS IMPROVEMENT: DISCUSSIONS AND ACTIONS

		How should we engage in discussions about the overarching work and performance of the PLC+ team in a spirit of continuous improvement?			
		When			
	Before Meetings	✓	During Meetings		After Meetings
		How Often			
	Planning	✓	Implementation		Reflection

Strategy in Action | Discussions and Actions

qrs.ly/gdgpggq

STRATEGY-AT-A-GLANCE

Continuous improvement in PLC+ teams requires purposeful reflection, candid analysis of results, and actionable next steps that align with team goals and student learning needs. This strategy supports teams in embedding a mindset of continuous growth by systematically identifying what's working, what isn't, and what can be done differently. Through regular, structured check-ins and evidence-informed reflections, activators help their teams maintain momentum and remain student centered. When implemented effectively, this strategy transforms reflection into progress and reshapes challenges into catalysts for meaningful instructional improvement.

RECOGNIZING THE NEED

During a midyear PLC+ meeting, Ms. Bennett looks around the table and asks, "Are we actually seeing any changes in how our students are learning, or are we just going through the motions?"

Mr. Rivera responds, "We've been meeting weekly, but I don't think we've really reflected on whether our PLC+ plan, overall, is working for our team."

Ms. Shah adds, "I think we need to pause and look at our data again—we might be holding onto routines that aren't moving learning forward."

Their activator, Mr. Collins, nods and says, "I agree. We've done a great job of responding to the five PLC+ questions to guide our work. But let's use this week to reflect on our entire PLC+ effort thus far. We can consider what's working and what's not, commit to a few focused changes to the way we are implementing the work, and then implement the changes before the next cycle begins."

ACTIVATING WITH THIS STRATEGY

Although PLC+ work is framed around investigation cycles that are guided by five key questions, maintaining progress across cycles demands a culture of reflection and refinement. Even highly functioning teams may default to comfortable practices rather than examining impact and adjusting course. Without intentional space for reflection, the PLC+ journey can stagnate. Using this strategy, activators can prompt thoughtful, nondefensive dialogue that leads to targeted improvement.

Approach	How to Activate
Routine Reflection	Schedule intentional reflection moments every four to six weeks, aligned with the investigation cycle. Prompt discussion around what has changed and what has improved.
The Five Guiding Questions	Anchor discussions in the PLC+ five guiding questions, especially Questions 4 and 5: *"What did we learn today?"* and *"Who benefited and who did not benefit?"*
Evidence-Based Dialogue	Use multiple forms of evidence—assessment data, student work, teacher feedback, and observations—to inform and focus conversations.
Celebrations and Adaptations	Highlight small wins and areas needing change. Frame improvement efforts around shared responsibility and student learning, not individual shortcomings.
Next-Steps Planning	Turn reflections into revised action steps. Assign roles and timelines for implementing adjustments before the next PLC+ cycle or lesson sequence.

SUCCESS CHECKLIST

✓	**Activation Task**
	Note Potential Challenges
☐	Patterns of discussion repeat without resulting in actionable change.
☐	There are missed opportunities to connect data or student work to instructional decisions.
☐	The PLC+ team shows reluctance to revise strategies or acknowledge areas needing improvement.
	Activate
☐	Schedule regular reflection points aligned with PLC+ inquiry cycles.
☐	Use the five guiding PLC+ questions, particularly Questions 4 and 5, to structure reflective discussions.
☐	Document agreed-upon changes and track follow-through using a shared log or planning tool.
	Reflect and Refine
☐	How are the team's current practices influencing student learning outcomes?
☐	What adjustments has the team made based on what the group has learned—and what results have they produced?
☐	How can the team better respond when students do not benefit from their instruction?

Notes

_____
_____
_____
_____
_____
_____
_____
_____
_____
_____
_____
_____
_____

14. CONTINUOUS IMPROVEMENT: MAKING COURSE CORRECTIONS

How does our PLC+ team make sure we remain on track to have a positive and predictable impact on teaching and learning?					
When					
	Before Meetings	✓	During Meetings		After Meetings
How Often					
	Planning	✓	Implementation		Reflection

Strategy in Action | Making Course Corrections

qrs.ly/9cgpggu

STRATEGY-AT-A-GLANCE

Remaining on a course for positive and predictable impact is a primary goal for any PLC+ effort. Activators should regularly review the team's progress, including comparing the work to date against what was planned. Based on this review, teams may choose to continue forward, make adjustments to the plan, or revise the plan more generally to hasten PLC+ impact. When the team needs to adjust their plans, they discuss and agree upon course corrections.

RECOGNIZING THE NEED

At a Wednesday afternoon PLC+ meeting, Mr. Carter, who has become concerned, shares, "I know we've stuck to the plan, but—clearly—something isn't working: Our students aren't showing growth."

Ms. Delgado glances at the latest assessment results and sighs. She says, "We've been so focused on fidelity to our methods that we forgot to listen to what the data—and the students—are actually telling us."

Mr. Lee nods slowly, adding, "Maybe it's time we stop measuring success by how well we follow our routine and start measuring it by how well our students are doing."

That day, the team agrees to rework their strategies, guided not by tradition but by the evolving needs of their learners.

ACTIVATING WITH THIS STRATEGY

It has been said that change is the only constant in life. Even the best laid plans may need revisions as they are implemented and monitored. Changes may be required due to unanticipated challenges, new opportunities, or changing priorities. In these cases, a course correction is necessary. Teams must carefully monitor their progress against the PLC+ plan while also using data to confirm that their direction of travel is effective and leading to impact. When that isn't the case, it may be time to change course or correct the course.

Here is a quick exercise that activators can try with the PLC+ team to reflect collaboratively on the PLC+ journey and path of travel. For this exercise, the team thinks of their work visually as a sequence of dots guiding their way toward defined outcomes and impact (Marshall, 2023), and then they record the steps they have completed.

1. Think back: How has the path to date allowed us to reach this point?
2. Is this the point we wanted to reach?
3. Think forward: Is the established path still pointing in a productive direction, toward accomplishments and outcomes that remain meaningful for us to achieve?
4. If not, what do we need to change: the pathway, the outcomes, or the pathway and the outcomes?

As this exercise can reveal, following a certain set of dots may be leading the team to success, or those dots may need to become connected in new ways. Sometimes changing the dots is what is actually required.

Approach	How to Activate
Connecting the Dots	Maybe the team will find that the dots defining the journey simply aren't connecting. This is likely symptomatic of the PLC+ implementation. This finding typically means there needs to be more attention on the implementation details, perhaps even fidelity to the PLC+ process, such that things become more connected. This shift might even include making stronger connections among team members, especially if the team is new to working with one another.
Correcting the Dots	This finding points to the need to change the defined outcomes and, also likely, the need to revisit and revise the plan of travel to reach those outcomes. Challenge the team by helping them realize that the current course isn't predictably leading to the outcomes the group agreed were the priority. Then, work together to refine the implementation path and those outcomes that need to be addressed, revised, or eliminated.
Expanding the Dots	If the team believes they have reached the end of the road, remind them that the journey still continues. Expanding the dots should happen when new needs arise midjourney. Make note of the synergy between the newly arising needs and the current PLC+ work because it will be critical for the team to choose to expand the path of travel in a way that not only addresses the new needs but also continues to work toward the outcomes they are already pursuing.

SUCCESS CHECKLIST

✓	Activation Task
	Note Potential Challenges
☐	There is a lack of adaptability to changing student needs.
☐	Meetings feel productive but are not yielding student progress.
☐	There is a disconnection between set goals and actual student outcomes.
	Activate
☐	Regularly review and analyze student data for effectiveness.
☐	Revise your PLC+ plan, strategies, and interventions when needed.
☐	Ensure that alignment exists between effort and measurable student success.
	Reflect and Refine
☐	Are the team's strategies still relevant to the current student needs?
☐	Is the team measuring success by effort or actual student progress?
☐	Is the team's path leading to meaningful accomplishments and outcomes?

Notes

_____
_____
_____
_____
_____
_____
_____
_____
_____
_____
_____
_____
_____
_____
_____
_____

15. CONTINUOUS IMPROVEMENT: TAKING PRIORITY PRACTICES TO SCALE

How do I determine when a PLC+ effort is ready to scale and lead its expansion in a way that sustains impact, builds shared ownership, and adapts to new contexts?

When					
	Before Meetings		During Meetings	✓	After Meetings
How Often					
	Planning		Implementation	✓	Reflection

Strategy in Action | Taking Priority Practices to Scale

qrs.ly/uugpggx

STRATEGY-AT-A-GLANCE

Scaling a successful PLC+ effort involves more than replication—it requires a thoughtful, intentional approach rooted in readiness, leadership, and learning design. Effective scaling begins with clarity of vision, identification of local champions, and structures that support alignment and flexibility (Marshall, 2023). Done right, scaling builds collective ownership, deepens professional growth, and ensures broader and more sustainable impact across classrooms, teams, and schools.

RECOGNIZING THE NEED

At Ridgeview Middle's end-of-year celebration, Ms. Langston says, "This PLC+ work brought our team together—we've grown so much."

Mr. Ellis chimes in by adding, "Other teams keep asking how we've made this work—they want in."

The principal, Dr. Raynor, suggests, "If this is changing how we teach and learn here, maybe it's time to scale this with intention, not just enthusiasm."

This moment plants the seed for a strategic, thoughtful expansion inspired by shared success and guided by strong leadership.

ACTIVATING WITH THIS STRATEGY

Scaling should be based on adaptive leadership, the presence of early champions, and the development of simple, repeatable structures. Rather than transplanting every element of a successful PLC+ team, activators should focus on transferring the core principles, customizing implementation to suit new contexts while maintaining coherence.

Approach	How to Activate
Assess readiness for scaling.	Use evidence of sustained team success—such as high-functioning norms, documented impact, and distributed leadership—as indicators for readiness. Use structured reflection protocols to assess alignment with PLC+ principles.
Use storytelling to spark vision.	Have original team members share the story of their growth, highlighting mindsets, breakthroughs, and shared commitments. These narratives build trust, inspire belief, and invite others into the journey.
Identify and support local champions.	Seek out individuals who are enthusiastic and respected within their teams. Empower them to colead early efforts, model protocols, and facilitate professional learning aligned with the PLC+ framework.
Design for simple, flexible replication.	Start small. Design a phased rollout that introduces core PLC+ elements while allowing adaptations for school culture and time structures. Ensure that new teams receive consistent support and opportunities to collaborate.
Build continuous learning systems.	Establish cycles of feedback, reflection, and support. Use surveys, team interviews, and learning walks to monitor fidelity, surface tensions, and celebrate growth. Use what you learn to adjust and grow the initiative.

SUCCESS CHECKLIST

✓	Activation Task
	Note Potential Challenges
☐	There are few early signs of readiness, such as strong team cohesion, consistent protocols, and evidence of impact.
☐	There is a lack of genuine interest from other teams or leaders seeking to understand or replicate PLC+ success.
☐	There are structural or cultural differences between teams that affect scalability.
	Activate
☐	Facilitate storytelling sessions to share growth journeys and spark interest across teams.
☐	Identify and empower local champions to support early scaling efforts and provide peer coaching.
☐	Design and implement a phased rollout with structures for feedback, monitoring, and adjustment.
	Reflect and Refine
☐	How is the team ensuring that scaling efforts stay true to the core values of PLC+?
☐	Is the team creating feedback systems that genuinely inform and improve their expansion efforts?
☐	What additional supports might the team need to be able to foster success in new teams or sites?

Notes

16. CONTINUOUS IMPROVEMENT: STRONG TEAM STRUCTURES TO ACHIEVE HIGH FUNCTION

How do I build the structures and shared responsibilities my PLC+ team needs to collaborate effectively and operate at a high level?					
When					
✓	Before Meetings	✓	During Meetings		After Meetings
How Often					
✓	Planning	✓	Implementation		Reflection

STRATEGY-AT-A-GLANCE

By focusing on collaboration, shared leadership, goal setting, rigorous discourse, and continuous improvement, teams can establish a foundation for impactful work. High-functioning teams rely on trust, structure, and consistent protocols to ensure that everyone contributes meaningfully. This strategy is grounded in the work of Elisa MacDonald (2023) who identified key elements such as collaboration, shared leadership, and continuous improvement as essential to high-functioning teams.

RECOGNIZING THE NEED

At Sunrise Intermediate School, the sixth-grade math PLC+ meets weekly, but progress feels slow. Mr. Ellis often takes on most of the work while others stay quiet or disengaged. One day, Ms. Dorsey mentions that they seem to complete tasks but aren't sure if it is changing student outcomes. When their instructional coach asks, "What would it take to truly function as a team?" the group realizes structure and shared responsibility are missing pieces.

ACTIVATING WITH THIS STRATEGY

To become a high-functioning PLC+ team, members must commit to shared practices that support collaboration and trust. Based on MacDonald's (2023) research, five key characteristics support this transformation. The following table outlines actions for each area.

Approach	How to Activate
Collaboration	Create systems where every member shares responsibility for outcomes. Use norms, rotating roles, and structured protocols (e.g., think–pair–share, tuning protocols) to ensure equal participation and shared ownership.
Shared Leadership	Rotate facilitation roles and encourage leadership in data analysis, note-taking, and protocol facilitation. Empower members to take initiative and cocreate agendas or next steps.
Goal Setting and Attainment	Set Specific, Measurable, Achievable, Relevant, Time-bound (SMART) goals that are meaningful and measurable. Revisit these regularly and connect team discussions and decisions back to these goals.
Rigorous Discourse	Foster inquiry-based conversations using sentence stems or guided protocols. Push for analysis of instructional practices and invite respectful challenges to promote deeper thinking.
Continuous Improvement	Use real-time data to examine progress and adapt strategies. Schedule regular reflection points and track impact over time to guide next moves.

SUCCESS CHECKLIST

✓	Activation Task
	Note Potential Challenges
☐	Team members complete tasks in isolation or default to one leader.
☐	There is a lack of clarity about goals, roles, or next steps.
☐	Discussions are polite but surface level, without pushing practice.
	Activate
☐	Establish team norms and clarify roles to ensure shared responsibility.
☐	Use structured agendas with time for goal review and next steps.
☐	Encourage all members to share, lead, and contribute regularly.
	Reflect and Refine
☐	How clearly defined are the team's roles and goals?
☐	Is the group operating as a team, or just as a group of individuals?
☐	What's one structure the team can tighten to help the group function more effectively?

FUNCTION AND IMPACT

An Introduction to Function and Impact

qrs.ly/z5gpgh0

17. FUNCTION AND IMPACT: ACTIVATING OTHERS BY SHARING YOUR PLC+ SUCCESS

How do we strategically share our PLC+ story and success to amplify the work within our school or district?					
When					
	Before Meetings		During Meetings	✓	After Meetings
How Often					
	Planning	✓	Implementation	✓	Reflection

STRATEGY-AT-A-GLANCE

Gaining and maintaining support for your PLC+ from school and district leadership is critical to sustaining the effort and impact. Strategically sharing your PLC+ story and success involves crafting messaging with careful attention to the *who, what, why,* and *how* of the communication you'll deliver. Formal leaders are often the ones who lead the charge of professional learning and development initiatives. Keep them abreast of your team's successes so that they may be better equipped to guide other activators to increase their impact.

RECOGNIZING THE NEED

At Jefferson High, the PLC+ team has made remarkable strides in teacher development and student achievement, often sharing personal wins during casual conversations. Teachers speak excitedly about new strategies that have boosted engagement and improved outcomes in their classrooms. However, outside the group, few colleagues or administrators are aware of the powerful impact the team has made. Despite the potential to inspire schoolwide and district-wide growth, the PLC+ team's success story remains quietly contained within their circle.

ACTIVATING WITH THIS STRATEGY

George Szulanski (1996) observed that it takes, on average, a minimum of two years for new knowledge or best practice to become shared internally within an organization. Realizations, epiphanies, successes, and new innovations—all realized by the team through hard work and dedication—stand to benefit others in the school and district, yet the PLC+ success story so often goes untold. Adapted from Marshall (2024), the following approach will help you catch the attention of colleagues beyond the PLC+, get the word out, and allow others to benefit from your insight and success.

Component	Sharing Strategies
The Who	First, think strategically about the *who*. With whom do you want to share your PLC+-generated innovations and impacts? Here are some likely suspects: 1. School leaders (e.g., your principal) 2. District leaders (e.g., other principals, central office leaders, or regional leaders) 3. School peers (e.g., teachers at your site who aren't involved in your PLC+) 4. District peers (e.g., teachers across the district who stand to benefit from your PLC+ effort)
The What	Next, continue thinking strategically to determine the message and information you wish to share. Remember that the *who* or *whos* you've targeted will influence the *what*, the *how*, and the *why*. Consider the following purposes when defining the *what* of sharing PLC+ information: • Building general awareness of your PLC+ effort • Sharing accomplishments related to early implementation and promising results, including early wins • Celebrating evidence of impact among the PLC+ team members and their students • Sharing tools, resources, and insights created or realized by your PLC+ team to help others

The How	Select the best way or ways to disseminate your message, and then craft your messaging for that vehicle.
	• Consider opportunities:
	  ◦ PLC+ to PLC+ joint team meetings
	  ◦ Visits to other PLC+-implementing school sites
	  ◦ All-school faculty meetings
	  ◦ District-sponsored professional growth opportunities
	  ◦ Newsletters and other communication tools—within the school, and beyond the school
	  ◦ Conferences and professional organization meetings
	• Get strategic:
	  ◦ Often, you'll want to lead with headlines or sound bites that immediately capture your main message and motivate the receiver to engage further to understand; said another way, don't bury the lede.
	  ◦ Use data to catch attention and demonstrate value by integrating it into your headlines.
	  ◦ When sharing a resource or tool developed by your PLC+ that can benefit others, efficiently share details about its development and implementation, while also describing the impact your team has observed.

The Why	As we've stressed, the ultimate *why* is to activate others, especially those beyond your PLC+. By sharing your story, accomplishments, and impact, you add value to the PLC+ initiative, press for others to engage and benefit in similar ways, and ultimately expand the activation of impactful teaching and learning.

SUCCESS CHECKLIST

✓	Activation Task
	Note Potential Challenges
☐	An awareness gap exists because many in the school and district are unaware of PLC+ approaches and successes.
☐	The team lacks a strong connection with school and district leaders who may support and amplify PLC+ innovations.
☐	The team doesn't benefit nor address the fact that messages about PLC+ may be received in different ways by different audiences.
	Activate
☐	Determine which school and district leaders, peers, or colleagues should receive PLC+ insights.
☐	Develop sound bites and headlines that succinctly communicate PLC+ successes and impact that can be used in faculty meetings, district events, newsletters, conferences, and beyond.
☐	Support shared insights with compelling evidence (data) to demonstrate PLC+ impact and value.
	Reflect and Refine
☐	How has the PLC+, overall, changed instructional practices for the better?
☐	In what ways have student learning and engagement improved because of PLC+ efforts?
☐	What outcomes has the team achieved through the telling of your PLC+ story—and what is left to tell?

Notes

18. FUNCTION AND IMPACT: APPLYING EVALUATIVE THINKING

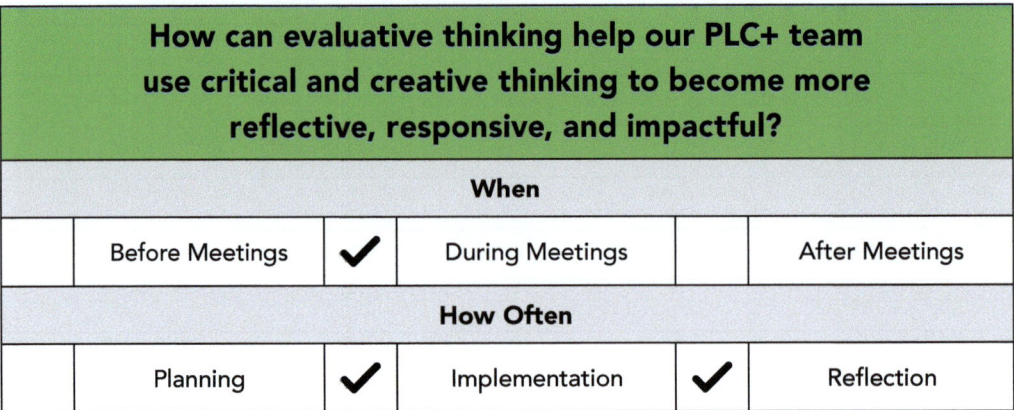

How can evaluative thinking help our PLC+ team use critical and creative thinking to become more reflective, responsive, and impactful?					
When					
	Before Meetings	✓	During Meetings		After Meetings
How Often					
	Planning	✓	Implementation	✓	Reflection

Strategy in Action | Applying Evaluative Thinking

qrs.ly/bxgpgh2

STRATEGY-AT-A-GLANCE

Embedding evaluative thinking into the daily practices of PLC+ teams drives continuous improvement. The approach is structured around key principles such as prioritizing evidence, seeking diverse perspectives, and iterating decisions based on data. When applied with intention, this strategy empowers educators to challenge assumptions, refine implementation, and maximize student outcomes.

RECOGNIZING THE NEED

It's Thursday afternoon at Hillcrest Middle School, and the PLC+ team gathers. Ms. Torres, the science teacher, says, "We've tried three strategies, but the engagement data still doesn't make sense."

Mr. Leland, the math teacher, replies, "Maybe we're looking at the wrong indicators or missing something in our implementation."

Ms. Nguyen adds, "What if our students don't understand the tasks the way we think they do?"

Mr. Evans, the instructional coach, leans in and asks, "What if it isn't the way we think it is?"

The room falls quiet as the team begins to explore how evaluative thinking could help them reframe assumptions and better understand their impact.

ACTIVATING WITH THIS STRATEGY

Evaluative thinking is the disciplined practice of applying critical and creative reasoning to program implementation and results. In the context of PLC+ teams, this mindset helps educators go beyond routine collaboration by embedding inquiry, evidence, and adaptability into their work. This strategy, adapted from Marshall (2024), centers on five core principles that guide teams through a cycle of planning, doing, reflecting, and improving.

Approach	How to Activate
Prioritize what's provable with evidence.	PLC+ teams commit to grounding their conversations and decisions in credible, diverse data—qualitative and quantitative. Rather than relying solely on intuition, teams examine trends, test assumptions, and seek evidence of effectiveness.
Pursue 360-degree viewpoints.	Team members actively seek insights from various stakeholders, including students, parents, and support staff. They recognize that multiple perspectives enrich understanding and surface blind spots in program design or delivery.
Press to understand process and outcome.	Teams investigate not just what results are occurring but also why and how. They analyze implementation fidelity, look for unintended effects, and draw links between practices and outcomes while acknowledging the complexity of causation.
Conclude, then disprove.	Once conclusions are drawn, teams apply skepticism to test the strength of their interpretations. They explore alternate explanations and challenge themselves to disprove their assumptions in the interest of truth and growth.
Make informed decisions—then do it again and again.	Teams make evidence-based decisions, act on them, and return to evaluate their impact. This iterative approach ensures that the PLC+ team evolves and adapts as new learning occurs.

PLC+ teams can integrate evaluative thinking into their regular meeting protocols. Each session might include a reflection on assumptions, a review of relevant data, a scan of stakeholder input, and a structured inquiry into the relationship between practice and impact. Using tools such as the Evaluative Thinking Checklist or guiding questions tied to the five principles, teams can remain agile, focused, and aligned with student-centered goals. Over time, this mindset cultivates a culture where curiosity, evidence, and improvement are the norm—not the exception.

SUCCESS CHECKLIST

✓	Activation Task
	Note Potential Challenges
☐	Assumptions go unspoken or unchallenged during team discussions.
☐	There are gaps or inconsistencies in the data being reviewed.
☐	Patterns of decision making are not adjusted despite new evidence.
	Activate
☐	Regularly incorporate diverse data sources (quantitative and qualitative) in PLC+ conversations.
☐	Invite and document perspectives from multiple stakeholders to enrich understanding.
☐	Create space in every meeting to revisit previous conclusions and refine next steps based on new insights.
	Reflect and Refine
☐	What assumptions is the team making about the students, and how can the group test those assumptions?
☐	Is the team considering all the voices and perspectives that matter in this situation?
☐	How does the team know that the change they're seeing is directly tied to what they implemented?

Notes

19. FUNCTION AND IMPACT: ASSESSING PLC+ READINESS

Are we, as a school site and potential PLC+ team, ready to engage in PLC+ work?					
When					
✓	Before Meetings		During Meetings		After Meetings
How Often					
✓	Planning		Implementation		Reflection

Strategy in Action | Assessing PLC+ Readiness

qrs.ly/j2gpgh6

STRATEGY-AT-A-GLANCE

Determining the starting point is an important aspect of planning a journey. You have to know where you are to plan where you are going, which mirrors the first two questions in the PLC+ model. *Your Introduction to PLC+* includes a readiness assessment you can use to investigate a range of research-based elements whose presence supports an effective PLC+. Understanding areas of strength—and areas of opportunity—will help you anticipate and plan the PLC+ work ahead.

RECOGNIZING THE NEED

During a planning session, Mr. Huynh glances around the table and says, "We've had PLCs for years, but I'm not sure we've ever stopped to ask if we're really ready for PLC+."

Ms. Carter replies, "The readiness assessment from the PLC+ guide could help us figure that out—it'll show us what we're doing well and where we need to grow."

Mr. Davis adds, "It makes sense; if we don't know where we stand, how can we plan for where we're going?"

With that, the team agrees to begin with the assessment, knowing it will provide the clarity and direction needed for meaningful collaboration and lasting impact.

ACTIVATING WITH THIS STRATEGY

Shirley Hord (1980) observed that cooperative teams can be less successful than collaborative teams because their members may divide tasks and work independently, each responsible for a specific piece of the whole. In contrast, collaborative teams engage in ongoing, interdependent work toward a common challenge. They build shared knowledge, examine data together, and engage in reflective dialogue, continuously adjusting their strategies based on insights from the group. Hord uses this metaphor: "Dating is a cooperative venture, while marriage is a collaborative one" (p. 6).

Figure 19.1: Needs Assessment Tool From *Your Introduction to PLC+*

NEEDS ASSESSMENT

Use this form to explore your readiness for a PLC+ initiative. Consider each of the five indicators and your school's or district's past efforts. Then, select a point on the scale that represents your current capacity, experience, or readiness to fulfill what each indicator describes.

	Our planned PLC+ initiative will be supported by:	Nothing in Place	Not a Current Strength	Some Demonstrated Capacity	Demonstrated Capacity in Place	Exemplary Capacity in Place
1.1	Dedicated PLC+ teams who engage the right people.	1	2	3	4	5
1.2	Dedicated time that is provided each week, at a minimum, for meetings that solely focus on the PLC+ initiative.	1	2	3	4	5
1.3	Access to necessary resources, such as shared technology, collaboration tools, and so on, that make the PLC+ work efficient and effective.	1	2	3	4	5
1.4	Access to the appropriate data, in usable formats, that support the PLC+ initiative's focus.	1	2	3	4	5
1.5	Access to disaggregated data in pursuit of understanding strengths and needs based on student performance over time.	1	2	3	4	5

Source: Fisher, D., & Frey, N. (2025). *Your introduction to PLC+*. Corwin.

Your activation work with this strategy involves using the Needs Assessment Tool, influenced by Hord's research, which is included in *Your Introduction to PLC+* (Fisher & Frey, 2025, see pp. 205–228).

1. With a new effort, or the switch from PLC to PLC+, use the Needs Assessment version of the tool to review each of the six research-based domains that correlate to PLC+-conducive settings.
2. Use the tool to identify current capacity, as well as elements that are not yet in place to support the PLC+.
3. Come to a consensus with your team for each rating assigned.
4. Finally, review the topography of your findings by recognizing the highs and the lows. Then discuss ways to leverage the strengths as well as what you will need to change to make a PLC+ conducive environment.

SUCCESS CHECKLIST

✓	Activation Task
	Note Potential Challenges
☐	The activator has not considered the difference between cooperative and collaborative teams.
☐	There are potential gaps in team readiness.
☐	The activator has not identified strengths already in place that the team can build on.
	Activate
☐	Identify strengths and gaps in PLC+ readiness using the Needs Assessment Tool.
☐	Reach a team consensus on assessment ratings.
☐	Develop strategies to leverage strengths and address weaknesses.
	Reflect and Refine
☐	How does the team currently function—cooperatively or collaboratively?
☐	What are the biggest obstacles to collaboration and PLC+ success?
☐	How can shared knowledge and data analysis improve team effectiveness?

20. FUNCTION AND IMPACT: ASSESSING YOUR CURRENT PLC+ PERFORMANCE

	How can I determine my PLC+ current performance level?				
	When				
	Before Meetings		During Meetings	✓	After Meetings
	How Often				
	Planning	✓	Implementation	✓	Reflection

STRATEGY-AT-A-GLANCE

You're familiar with the five PLC+ leading questions. Whether you're beginning the work or you have been at it for a time, there is always an opportunity to reflect on your current capacity. Completing the Self-Assessment Tool in *Your Introduction to PLC+* will help you identify strengths already in place, as well as the elements you may need to address to activate the way forward.

RECOGNIZING THE NEED

Hawthorne Elementary's upper elementary PLC+ team of fourth- and fifth-grade teachers, who meet regularly to discuss all things teaching and learning, has been in place for more than half of the school year. Up to this point, the team has enjoyed early success and the opportunity to come together. However, now that they've reached the middle of the school year, interest appears to be fading. Attendance has become less regular, and conversations feel shallower. Some teachers are even suggesting the work is done.

One teacher activator on the team decides to address the situation she has begun to see week after week. She challenges the team by asking, "Have we gotten off track in using the five PLC+ questions intentionally and consistently to guide our PLC+ work?"

Figure 20.1: Self-Assessment Tool From *Your Introduction to PLC+*

SELF-ASSESSMENT

Use the following five statements, one per essential question, for rapid assessment. Read the question and corresponding statement, and then discuss your current state with your PLC+ team. Come to a shared agreement about the current capacity and implementation for each statement.

1. Notice: Where Are We Going?

   We define our expectations through learning intentions and success criteria, and these definitions involve learning progressions over time, moving to the point of equity of access and opportunity for learning for all students.

1	2	3	4	5
Not Begun or Not Initiated	Very Limited Evidence of Capacity	Some Evidence of Capacity	Evidence of Capacity and Limited Evidence of Effective Implementation	Evidence of Capacity and Demonstrated Effective Implementation

   Reflect: Who is "in the know" about our expectations? How have our processes made space for students, families, and educators to co-construct and/or understand these expectations? What do we believe about how much these groups should contribute to defining our expectations?

2. Notice: Where Are We Now?

   We collect and analyze evidence to understand our students, identify equity gaps, challenge bias, and define common challenges that unite our efforts and support collective efficacy.

1	2	3	4	5
Not Begun or Not Initiated	Very Limited Evidence of Capacity	Some Evidence of Capacity	Evidence of Capacity and Limited Evidence of Effective Implementation	Evidence of Capacity and Demonstrated Effective Implementation

   Reflect: What evidence do we collect? What does this evidence support us to see? What are the limitations of this evidence in supporting us to see the unique interests, skills, and talents that our students possess and opportunities to build from those assets in our work to support learners?

3. Notice: How Do We Move Learning Forward?

   We match evidence-based instructional approaches to defined learning needs, assess and increase our own abilities to deliver instruction, and use learning walks and microteaching to move learning forward.

(Continued)

(Continued)

1	2	3	4	5
Not Begun or Not Initiated	Very Limited Evidence of Capacity	Some Evidence of Capacity	Evidence of Capacity and Limited Evidence of Effective Implementation	Evidence of Capacity and Demonstrated Effective Implementation

Reflect: How do make decisions about instructional moves? In what ways do we learn from others about effective practices? How do we draw from Black, Indigenous, and other minoritized and marginalized communities to learn culturally responsive and relevant instructional approaches? Do we believe that we can benefit from these perspectives?

4. Notice: What Did We Learn Today?

   We regularly examine our practice, discuss expectations, identify and act on student needs, and seek to describe elements of our practice that yield, or do not yield, a measurable, positive impact.

1	2	3	4	5
Not Begun or Not Initiated	Very Limited Evidence of Capacity	Some Evidence of Capacity	Evidence of Capacity and Limited Evidence of Effective Implementation	Evidence of Capacity and Demonstrated Effective Implementation

Reflect: How do we understand student needs? What processes do we have that support students to articulate their needs and provide feedback about how our curriculum and pedagogy meet their needs? How do students know we've heard them?

5. Notice: Who Benefited and Who Did Not?

   We intentionally seek to identify patterns that suggest barriers to learning, monitor progress and achievement for all students, and modify instruction using strategies that include tiered systems, new approaches to instruction, and heightening collective efficacy.

1	2	3	4	5
Not Begun or Not Initiated	Very Limited Evidence of Capacity	Some Evidence of Capacity	Evidence of Capacity and Limited Evidence of Effective Implementation	Evidence of Capacity and Demonstrated Effective Implementation

Reflect: Whose voices have been invited to seek patterns? What might we learn from engaging paraprofessionals, after-school staff, students, and families if we invited them to help identify patterns? What fears or reservations might we be holding in inviting these perspectives? What structural barriers need to be addressed in order to engage these groups authentically?

Source: Fisher, D., & Frey, N. (2025). *Your introduction to PLC+*. Corwin.

ACTIVATING WITH THIS STRATEGY

Your Introduction to PLC+ includes a helpful assessment tool that is made for the type of situation faced by the Hawthorne Elementary team; this tool will also benefit your own activator efforts. The assessment covers each of the five PLC+ questions and challenges you and your PLC+ team to reflect on your current practice—as a PLC+ team and in implementing teaching and learning—at regular points in the journey. Use this tool to guide these actions:

- Review your current practice.
- Compare ratings over time by taking regular pulse checks at least three times a year.
- Prompt meaningful discussion around your PLC+ effort in terms of alignment to the five questions and the recommended PLC+ practices they each involve.

Use the following table to track your question-by-question ratings and planned actions over time.

Question	Beginning of Year	Mid-Year Check-In	End-of-Year Reflection
Question 1: Where are we going?			
Comments and planned actions based on findings:			
Question 2: Where are we now?			
Comments and planned actions based on findings:			
Question 3: How do we move things forward?			
Comments and planned actions based on findings:			

(Continued)

(Continued)

Question	Beginning of Year	Mid-Year Check-In	End-of-Year Reflection
Question 4: What did we learn today?			
Comments and planned actions based on findings:			
Question 5: Who benefited and who did not benefit?			
Comments and planned actions based on findings:			

SUCCESS CHECKLIST

✓	Activation Task
Note Potential Challenges	
☐	There is declining attendance in PLC+ meetings, and team members question the relevance of the PLC+ work.
☐	There are shallow or disengaged conversations.
☐	There is a lack of intentional use of the PLC+ framework.
Activate	
☐	Use the PLC+ assessment tool to evaluate team progress.
☐	Schedule regular reviews at least three times a year to provide accountability for the team.
☐	Facilitate discussions aligning PLC+ work with the five key questions.
Reflect and Refine	
☐	Is the team consistently using the PLC+ framework?
☐	How has the team's engagement changed over time?
☐	How do the team's discussions align with effective PLC+ practices?

21. FUNCTION AND IMPACT: BUILDING MOMENTUM WITH EARLY WINS

How do I help my PLC+ team gain early momentum and build confidence by defining, achieving, and celebrating early wins?					
When					
	Before Meetings	✓	During Meetings		After Meetings
How Often					
✓	Planning	✓	Implementation		Reflection

STRATEGY-AT-A-GLANCE

Early wins provide an effective strategy to build, engage, and motivate PLC+ teams. They signal to educators that change is possible and progress is underway, helping to shift mindsets and motivate continued effort. By identifying short-term, meaningful accomplishments, PLC+ teams can create a positive feedback loop that drives sustainable improvement.

RECOGNIZING THE NEED

At Lincoln Elementary, the fourth-grade PLC+ has just launched a new reading initiative, and the energy in the room is low. Ms. Boyd, usually upbeat, expresses doubt, saying, "We've tried things before, and nothing ever sticks."

Mr. Daniels adds, "It feels like a mountain—we don't even know if we're climbing in the right direction."

Just then, their instructional coach asks, "What's one thing we've already done right?"

That question sparks a shift—and a new focus on small, early wins to reignite their belief in the work.

ACTIVATING WITH THIS STRATEGY

Jody Spiro (2012) defines *early wins* as "successes demonstrating concretely that achieving the change goals is feasible and will result in benefits for those involved" (p. 10). In PLC+ teams, early wins create confidence, build momentum, and motivate members to stay the course. The following table outlines how activators can help their PLC+ team define, pursue, and celebrate early wins as part of their collaborative improvement work.

Approach	How to Activate
Define early wins.	Work with your PLC+ team to identify short-term, tangible goals that are achievable within the first few meetings or phases of an initiative. These should be aligned to broader goals but broken into small successes—such as 100 percent attendance at a first meeting, submission of baseline data, or completion of one shared lesson plan.
Pursue and document.	Create tools such as shared goal trackers, meeting notes templates, or visual progress charts (picture the thermometer used to track fund-raising, as an example) to monitor early win progress. Encourage team members to reflect on what led to these accomplishments and how they contribute to overall growth. Make success visible and part of team language.
Celebrate and share.	Take time to recognize early wins in meaningful ways—such as shout-outs during meetings, recognition boards, or messages from leadership. Explain why each early win matters and connect it to long-term goals. Use early wins to establish a narrative of progress, collective efficacy, and shared ownership.

SUCCESS CHECKLIST

✓	Activation Task
	Note Potential Challenges
☐	There is low team morale or skepticism about new initiatives.
☐	Discussions lack the benefit of a mindset shift, such as when a positive or reflective question changes the tone of a conversation.
☐	There are few opportunities to recognize progress, even small ones, which can signal change and motivate continued effort.
	Activate
☐	Collaborate with your PLC+ team to define short-term, tangible early win goals that align with broader objectives.
☐	Use tools like trackers, templates, or visual progress charts to document and monitor progress on early wins.
☐	Celebrate early wins publicly in meaningful ways and connect them to the long-term vision and team success.
	Reflect and Refine
☐	What early wins has the team already achieved, and how did they impact team motivation and mindset?
☐	How do the team's current early win strategies align with the broader goals and desired outcomes?
☐	What systems or supports could help the team better recognize, document, and celebrate the progress?

22. FUNCTION AND IMPACT: EVALUATING YOUR PLC+ PROGRESS AND IMPACT

How should we evaluate the work and success of our PLC+ effort?					
When					
	Before Meetings		During Meetings	✓	After Meetings
How Often					
	Planning	✓	Implementation	✓	Reflection

STRATEGY-AT-A-GLANCE

Continuous improvement in PLC+ teams relies on clear goals, intentional planning, and regular reflection. This strategy highlights the need to identify outcomes, define success indicators, and establish ways to measure progress. Instead of relying on anecdotes or enthusiasm, teams use evidence-informed cycles of review and adjustment. Activators help guide the process, celebrate early wins, and make data-driven changes. With consistent use, this approach keeps PLC+ work focused and impactful.

RECOGNIZING THE NEED

The Blaine High School English department forms a PLC+ with the goal of improving student writing. Excited to collaborate, they meet regularly, discussing ideas and sharing resources. However, they never define specific outcomes, assuming their collective enthusiasm will naturally lead to progress. They implement various strategies—peer editing one week, grammar drills the next—but without a clear focus or method to track success, their efforts feel scattered. Meetings become repetitive, with teachers sharing anecdotes rather than analyzing concrete results. Months pass, and when asked about their impact, they have no data to show whether students have improved. Frustration grows as some question whether their work has made any difference.

ACTIVATING WITH THIS STRATEGY

Evaluating your progress begins by having a carefully defined and documented process. Think of it as a direction of travel with clear stops along the way and identified indicators by which your progress and accomplishments will be assessed and celebrated. Activators take an active role in defining the PLC+ team's work, while also adjusting it—when necessary—over time.

Evaluation, at the most basic level, means documenting and reflecting upon the PLC+ team's progress in reaching outcomes. This includes short-term outcomes (e.g., holding to the meeting schedule, implementing agreed lessons in the classroom, conducting learning walks, analyzing data according to the assessment calendar), and longer-term outcomes (e.g., changes in teaching practice over time, changes in student performance, evidence of growth). Thus, for evaluation to happen, your PLC+ plan must have defined goals and outcomes, and you must agree on what you'll accept as evidence of reaching those goals and outcomes. With that clarity realized, you then monitor progress against your plan and outcomes, and you regularly check in with the team along the way.

We suggest you set incremental milestones that everyone can do and celebrate. As the previous strategy described, these early wins can build momentum while uniting a newly formed team in purpose. Holding the first successful meeting, establishing roles, establishing norms, implementing the first lesson, and analyzing the first pieces of data are all examples of early wins you should plan into your PLC+ work, monitor, document upon achievement, and celebrate.

At the highest level, your evaluation effort should include the following elements.

Approach	How to Activate
Define goals and outcomes.	Identify short- and long-term goals your PLC+ team aims to achieve. Clarify expected changes in practice and student outcomes and document them in your team plan.
Determine evidence of success.	Agree on what counts as evidence for each goal. This may include student work samples, assessment results, meeting logs, observation notes, or instructional artifacts.
Establish milestones and monitor progress.	Break goals into achievable steps—or early wins—that the team can celebrate. Use regular check-ins to assess progress and make data-informed adjustments to the plan.

You should also regularly share your progress with your peers, site leadership, and district team.

SUCCESS CHECKLIST

✓	Activation Task
	Note Potential Challenges
☐	There is a lack of clearly defined outcomes, which is leading to unfocused efforts.
☐	PLC+ team members are frustrated due to an absence of measurable progress.
☐	The team's efforts feel scattered and lack a method to track success.
	Activate
☐	Define clear goals and outcomes for the PLC+ team and implement a structured method for tracking progress and success.
☐	Set incremental milestones (early wins) to build momentum.
☐	Regularly share progress with peers, leadership, and district teams.
	Reflect and Refine
☐	How well is the team aligning the efforts with the defined outcomes?
☐	Is the team collecting and analyzing concrete data to measure progress?
☐	Are there planned accomplishments just ahead that could be made into early wins to support the team's momentum and motivation?

Notes

_____
_____
_____
_____
_____
_____
_____
_____
_____
_____
_____
_____
_____

23. FUNCTION AND IMPACT: INCREASING IMPACT IN PLC+ TEAMS

How do I help my PLC+ team focus deeply on student learning and ensure that our collaboration leads to measurable impact?					
When					
	Before Meetings	✓	During Meetings		After Meetings
How Often					
✓	Planning	✓	Implementation	✓	Reflection

Strategy in Action | Increasing Impact in PLC+ Teams

qrs.ly/ojgpgh9

STRATEGY-AT-A-GLANCE

Teams often appear productive but miss the deeper interdependence and reflection required to truly impact student learning. With clarity, trust, and a shared commitment to results, teams can reach their highest potential. Drawing on Elisa MacDonald's (2023) framework, this approach focuses on moving beyond surface-level productivity toward meaningful impact on student learning.

RECOGNIZING THE NEED

At Maple Valley High, the English PLC+ is known for its organized meetings and impressive charts. Still, Ms. Yates notices that student outcomes aren't improving, and Mr. Collins admits, "We meet often, but I'm not sure we're actually changing anything."

Then the newest member of the PLC+ asks, "How do we know we're making a difference?"

This question sparks an honest reflection. They realize they have the structure but haven't achieved the impact they are seeking.

ACTIVATING WITH THIS STRATEGY

High-impact PLC+ teams reflect deeply and adjust intentionally based on what they learn. The following strategies help teams shift from compliance to transformation by focusing on results, trust, and collaborative effort.

Approach	How to Activate
Revisit impact questions.	At every meeting, use reflection prompts such as *"What did we learn today?"* or *"What changed for students as a result of our work?"* Make student learning the anchor of all PLC+ conversations.
Build relational trust.	Create a safe space where vulnerability is welcome. Encourage teammates to share challenges without fear of judgment and to listen actively to one another.
Celebrate small wins.	Document progress visibly (e.g., progress walls or shared dashboards). Acknowledge contributions, improvements, and experimentation during team meetings.
Push for depth.	Use protocols like the 5 Whys or Success Analysis to go beyond surface-level problem solving. Promote reflective questioning and deeper analysis of data and instructional practices.
Identify shared challenges.	Engage the team in identifying a common problem of practice. Collaboratively set a learning goal and develop strategies to test and reflect on its impact.

SUCCESS CHECKLIST

✓	Activation Task
	Note Potential Challenges
☐	Teams look organized but have limited student impact.
☐	Teams repeat tasks without real discussion or change.
☐	One or two members are doing most of the heavy lifting.
	Activate
☐	Refocus meetings on learning, not just logistics or data reporting.
☐	Use protocols to examine student work and instructional impact.
☐	Support team members in co-owning the responsibility for student outcomes.
	Reflect and Refine
☐	What evidence does the team have that the collaboration is improving learning?
☐	Is the team truly learning from one another?
☐	How can the team deepen the conversations and commitments to student success?

24. FUNCTION AND IMPACT: REALIZING THE OPTIMAL COMBINATION OF FUNCTION AND IMPACT

How do I integrate strong team function with a relentless focus on impact so that my PLC+ team can transform teaching and learning?					
When					
	Before Meetings	✓	During Meetings		After Meetings
How Often					
✓	Planning	✓	Implementation		Reflection

STRATEGY-AT-A-GLANCE

This strategy focuses on the integration of high function and high impact to build truly transformative PLC+ teams. Grounded in the research of Elisa MacDonald (2023), it combines the essential structures of effective collaboration with a relentless focus on student-learning outcomes. When function and impact work in tandem, PLC+ teams are positioned to drive meaningful, sustainable improvement in adult practice and student achievement.

RECOGNIZING THE NEED

At Lakewood Middle School, the seventh-grade multidisciplinary PLC+ is active and collegial—but unsure if their work is making a difference. Mr. Khalil notices that their well-run meetings lack the deeper analysis of student outcomes, while Ms. Rivera observes that their shared challenges rarely lead to shared solutions. Frustration grows when efforts don't seem to lead to change, despite the group's strong relationships. The team realizes they need not just effective structures, but also a renewed focus on the real impact of their work.

ACTIVATING WITH THIS STRATEGY

High-functioning, high-impact PLC+ teams do more than meet efficiently—they transform teaching and learning. Combining structure and trust with a deep focus on outcomes ensures that collaborative work translates into meaningful student growth. The following table outlines strategies that bridge both elements and promote excellence across the team.

Approach	How to Activate
Establish shared goals.	Align instructional goals with team and school priorities. Make goal progress a recurring agenda item and ensure alignment with student data and needs.
Balance voices and leadership.	Use facilitation strategies (e.g., protocols, talking chips, or turn taking) to ensure that every voice is heard. Encourage distributed leadership through planning and data analysis roles.
Make student learning visible.	Examine student work using collaborative protocols and tie observations to instructional adjustments. Celebrate student growth and track patterns across classrooms.
Create a culture of challenge.	Normalize disagreement and feedback as growth opportunities. Encourage team members to question assumptions, revisit decisions, and reflect collectively.
Celebrate progress and adjust often.	Make time to reflect on wins, however small, and adjust approaches based on current student evidence. Use short cycles of inquiry to guide changes and document learning.

SUCCESS CHECKLIST

✓	Activation Task
	Note Potential Challenges
☐	Teams operate well logistically but lack evidence of student growth.
☐	There is resistance to feedback, or there is discomfort with deep, reflective conversations.
☐	There is an uneven distribution of participation or ownership across the team.
	Activate
☐	Establish norms that support collaboration and accountability.
☐	Create meeting agendas that balance structure with reflection and impact analysis.
☐	Build team capacity to navigate discomfort and embrace honest dialogue.
	Reflect and Refine
☐	How well do the team's structures support the desired outcomes?
☐	Does the team consistently link their collaboration to changes in student learning?
☐	What's one way the team can improve how they work and the results they achieve?

MEETING MOVES

An Introduction to
Meeting Moves

qrs.ly/m4gpgha

25. MEETING MOVES: COMING TO AGREEMENT ABOUT PROFESSIONAL LEARNING

How do I lead my PLC+ team toward meaningful professional learning that feels relevant, reduces resistance, and supports improved teaching and learning?					
When					
	Before Meetings	✔	During Meetings		After Meetings
How Often					
	Planning	✔	Implementation		Reflection

STRATEGY-AT-A-GLANCE

Developing teacher effectiveness and expertise is one of the most critical ways the PLC+ work ultimately benefits each team member. Given such critical contributions, it is important to highlight how activators can lead the PLC+ team toward professional learning that is aligned with the PLC+ focus, meets the needs and complements the strengths of the PLC+ team, and ultimately transfers to classroom practice and student performance.

RECOGNIZING THE NEED

Bree Santiago, a member of a grade-one PLC+ team, notes that her colleagues do not agree on the professional learning needed within the PLC+ framework. She explains, "Some of my colleagues feel their degrees and experience have equipped them with all they need to be successful. In fact, one team member said that parents and principals need to do their part. In another meeting, another colleague announced, 'This educational jargon is not necessary. Plus, this is what we used to do in the eighties. Recycled ideas. Just wait and this will pass.'"

ACTIVATING WITH THIS STRATEGY

Let's acknowledge that the transition from talking about instruction to agreeing on professional learning can be a challenging one. As teams talk about instruction, the conversation about professional learning arises, but not everyone may agree that professional learning is a necessary part of the PLC+ effort. As an activator, how can you keep the team moving forward while also emphasizing the important contributions professional learning can make? The following table provides three strategies that have proven effective as professional-learning approaches.

Approach	How to Activate
Toss the jargon; pose the questions.	Consider tossing the jargon associated with professional learning. Realizing that word choice matters, consistently use words associated with student learning. In addition to the traditional approach of "telling," also use questions focused on student learning to guide the group's professional learning.
Unpack the meaning.	Concepts such as *formative assessment, differentiation, clarity, rigor,* and *efficacy,* to name a few, are not jargon. However, the meaning of those terms may not be clear to everyone. Although your approach may be met with resistance, devote some of the professional learning to unpacking what is meant by terms for which the group lacks a shared understanding.
Take the paperwork pledge.	In addition to suffering from initiative fatigue, teachers can suffer from too much administrative work. Consequently, the thought of *more* paperwork can be daunting. Make a personal commitment to members of the PLC+ team that the amount of PLC+ paperwork, including the paperwork associated with professional learning, will be minimal or less than the amount they currently do. In sum, work smarter, not harder.

SUCCESS CHECKLIST

✓	Activation Task
	Note Potential Challenges
☐	The PLC+ team is resistant to professional learning due to past experiences.
☐	The team expresses concerns about an additional workload from professional learning.
☐	There are diverging views on the necessity of professional learning.
	Activate
☐	Use student-focused language instead of jargon to guide discussions.
☐	Clarify and unpack key educational terms to ensure shared understanding.
☐	Ensure that professional learning aligns with team needs and strengths.
	Reflect and Refine
☐	How does professional learning impact student success?
☐	What strategies help in overcoming resistance to change?
☐	How can teachers balance professional growth with workload management?

26. MEETING MOVES: DOCUMENTATION AND NOTE-TAKING

What are the permanent products—notes—that a team should take to remember their decisions and planned actions?					
When					
	Before Meetings	✓	During Meetings		After Meetings
How Often					
	Planning	✓	Implementation		Reflection

STRATEGY-AT-A-GLANCE

Effective teams document their work and summarize the decisions they make so that they can refer to them over time. Notes, or meeting minutes, provide a written record of discussions, decisions, and action items, which helps ensure that everyone is on the same page, promotes transparency, and facilitates follow-up and accountability. These notes are often called *minutes*, a term that originates from the Latin *minuta scriptura*, meaning "small notes" or "rough draft," which reflects the idea that the notes a team takes are concise and focused in nature.

RECOGNIZING THE NEED

At Avalon Middle School, grade-level teams are the norm. These teams loop up through the grades with their students, from sixth to seventh to eighth and then back again with a new cohort of students. Teams consist of the English, history, science, mathematics, and special education teachers who teach the same students. The arts, physical education, and career and technical education teachers are also a team because they teach all the students in the school.

The notes that each team takes are shared with the other teams because the teachers will progress to the next grade level the following year. For example, during a meeting, one of the five current seventh-grade teams accesses the notes from a previous seventh-grade team (a group that is now teaching eighth grade). One of the current seventh-grade teachers, Maria Jimenez, says, "There is a really good assessment of their interdisciplinary project in the notes. Did you see the questions that the team said were too easy for the students? And the two questions that seemed to be confusing? We should review and maybe revise those items for this year."

Based on their structure, the teams access previous notes and contribute new notes to the overall PLC+ operating in their school.

ACTIVATING WITH THIS STRATEGY

One specific person should be designated as the recorder or note-taker for each team meeting. This can be decided at the outset of the meeting, or it can be planned in advance. All the team members should have access to the notes and be provided with opportunities to contribute, but one person should be designated as the primary person to record the information, decisions, and actions.

Approach	How to Activate
Capture the essence of the discussion.	Record the 5 As during the meeting: **Attendance:** who was there **Agenda:** what was discussed **Answers:** what questions were discussed **Agreements:** what was decided **Actions:** what needs to be completed If you are comfortable with audio recording the meeting, you can use generative artificial intelligence (AI) tools such as Otter, Rewatch, Fireflies, MeetGeek, Fellow, and Rev to optimize meetings. You can also use AI to summarize the notes (as discussed later in this section). Keep notes together, either in a shared folder or a file.
Choose a system for retention.	There are several systems that help the note-taker capture the necessary information—and different people may use different systems based on what works best for them. There is no single "right" way to take notes. Here is a useful list of some common systems. **Outline Method:** Ideal for breaking information into organized sections and subpoints. It's a structured approach that helps keep details in order with roman numbers and letters. **Sentence Method:** Best for those who prefer writing complete thoughts. This style captures information as full sentences, making it easier to recall the context later. **Charting Method:** A go-to for visual learners who benefit from seeing relationships laid out. Use columns to compare ideas, data, or steps side by side. **Cornell Note-Taking System:** Split your page into dedicated areas for cues, detailed notes, and a summary. This system is highly organized and simplifies reviewing complex material. **Mapping Method:** Great for visualizing ideas. Begin with a central topic and expand outward, connecting related points. Perfect for creative thinking and quick idea generation. **Quadrant Method:** Divide the page into four boxes labeled *Notes, Questions, To-Dos,* and *To Assign*. Ideal for managing personal tasks and team responsibilities during a meeting.

(Continued)

(Continued)

Approach	How to Activate
Summarize and organize notes later, not during the meeting.	Using a template can help with taking notes in real time because they provide a general structure that is prepopulated. Using the same template every time makes it easier for team members to find the information they need quickly. Templates also save time in meeting setup. As part of the process, meeting notes need to be summarized, but this should not occur during the meeting itself. Rather, the note-taker should plan to review and synthesize the notes after the meeting. Again, AI systems can easily provide the first draft of the summary and action items. A systematic approach involves the 4 Rs: **Record:** Write down key information, as noted above. **Reduce:** Synthesize key information, using keywords and ideas. **Reflect:** Think about the information and how it reflects the work of the team and the actions needed. **Review:** Look over notes periodically as a team.

SUCCESS CHECKLIST

✓	Activation Task
	Note Potential Challenges
☐	The 5 As (Attendance, Agenda, Answers, Agreements, Actions) are not being captured during each PLC+ meeting.
☐	A note-taker is not designated, and members do not all have access to contribute to or review the notes.
☐	The PLC+ team is not using note-taking systems effectively and consistently.
	Activate
☐	Designate a note-taker and adopt a common template.
☐	Choose a system for recording and sharing the notes that works for the team. Consider using AI tools.
☐	Actively refer to past meeting notes to inform current decisions and actions.
	Reflect and Refine
☐	How do the team's notes reflect the growth and learning as a team over time?
☐	Are team notes detailed enough to be a useful record of the discussion but not so detailed that the process is burdensome?
☐	Do all team members have access to, and regularly review, notes from the discussions? Are there follow-ups in subsequent meetings to the actions identified in the notes?

27. MEETING MOVES: EFFECTIVELY ACTIVATING WHEN MEETINGS BECOME CHALLENGING

> How do I navigate emotionally charged moments in PLC+ meetings in ways that honor all voices, uphold our shared values, and keep the team moving forward?

When					
	Before Meetings	✓	During Meetings		After Meetings
How Often					
	Planning	✓	Implementation		Reflection

Strategy in Action | Effectively Activating When Meetings Become Challenging

qrs.ly/7pgpghc

STRATEGY-AT-A-GLANCE

We have all been in a meeting where a contentious statement about students, families, colleagues, or equity made it challenging to have a productive conversation. This too can happen in a PLC+ setting. When it does, activators should assess the situation, then take actions, such as pausing the meeting, redirecting the conversation, and facilitating the team's processing of the situation. The goal for the activator is to navigate the challenging moments with grace and recognize that people have complex emotions that can arise when they care about the discussion.

RECOGNIZING THE NEED

Tension surfaces during a PLC+ meeting when Mr. Whitman comments, "These students just don't value education the way we did. They don't even do the practice work I assign."

Several team members go quiet. Then Ms. Hill gently responds, "I think we need to pause and consider how our assumptions might be impacting our expectations."

Mr. Reyes steps in to acknowledge the emotional weight in the room. He redirects the group to the community agreements—reminding the team that discomfort can be a sign that the group is on the edge of real growth.

Mr. Whitman responds, "Maybe students aren't completing the practice because they need more academic support. If I'm really honest, I didn't always do the work my teachers assigned. Our students really are just like us."

ACTIVATING WITH THIS STRATEGY

When meetings become challenging, keep the following strategies close by to help you lead the team through the conversation and challenge.

Approach	How to Activate
Assess the emotional tone and energy in the room (the group dynamic).	Do a quick scan of the room to assess other people's reactions to the comment. Look for nonverbal cues (e.g., facial expression, body language, gestures, hand raising, etc.).
Pause the meeting to name the tension in the room.	"It seems like there's a lot of strong emotion in the room. I want to name that it's normal for emotion to surface when discussing equity issues, and I want to make some space for you to work through whatever you're feeling before we continue our discussion."
Insert a pair–share to let people process the feelings that have come up.	"Take a moment, turn to a partner, and take five minutes each to share whatever feelings or thoughts have come up for you. Try to focus on what YOU are needing and feeling, as opposed to focusing on others."
Find something to affirm and validate what may be lying beneath the statement.	"It sounds like you have strong feelings about this, and I imagine that frustration comes from wanting something better for . . ." or "It sounds like you have some specific experiences with . . . that must be very challenging."
Find ways to redirect toward our core values and vision.	"I hear your frustration, and I want to remind us to stay connected to our core values as a community and to what's still possible for . . ." or "It's true that we have students and families who are struggling with these issues, but we need to be careful not to default to making generalizations . . ." or "Let's take a moment to use our community agreements to reflect on our group dynamic at this moment. . . . What do we need from one another to stay in community?" or "I bet this was not your intent, but that statement could be heard as [judging, hurtful, inflammatory]. . . . Do you want to clarify what you meant?"

Source: Tool developed by the National Equity Project

Be sure to follow up with individuals who are particularly affected—and the person who made the comment—after the meeting. Consider how you might address this topic in your next meeting.

SUCCESS CHECKLIST

✓	Activation Task
	Note Potential Challenges
☐	There are shifts in body language or tone that signal discomfort, frustration, or disengagement.
☐	Comments generalize or marginalize student groups—even if that is not the intention.
☐	Silence or hesitation follows a controversial or an emotionally charged statement.
	Activate
☐	Pause the conversation to acknowledge tension and create space for emotional processing.
☐	Redirect the dialogue toward shared PLC+ values and community agreements.
☐	Facilitate a reset through structured protocols (e.g., pair–share, norm review, recentering questions).
	Reflect and Refine
☐	How do you recognize when the emotional climate of the room needs attention?
☐	In what ways can you support team members in staying grounded in shared values during tense moments?
☐	How can you better prepare to respond to future moments of discomfort with empathy and clarity?

Notes

28. MEETING MOVES: ESTABLISHING NORMS

Why are norms important for the PLC+, and how do we go about establishing them?					
When					
	Before Meetings	✓	During Meetings		After Meetings
How Often					
✓	Planning	✓	Implementation		Reflection

Strategy in Action | Establishing Norms

qrs.ly/yfgpghe

STRATEGY-AT-A-GLANCE

Norms help PLC+ teams optimize their efficiency and effectiveness. Establishing norms can set expectations for things like respectful dialogue, shared responsibility, and structured agendas. With expectations in place, meetings become productive, collaboration can flourish, and impact can result.

RECOGNIZING THE NEED

At Oakwood Middle School, a group of enthusiastic teachers have formed a PLC+ but have skipped the crucial step of setting team norms. At first, things seem fine, but as meetings progress, tension grows. As meetings continue, conversations veer off-topic, some voices are silenced, and deadlines are missed. Frustration grows, conflicts remain unresolved, and participation begins to drop. Realizing the need for change, the team creates clear norms, leading to more productive meetings, better collaboration, and meaningful progress.

ACTIVATING WITH THIS STRATEGY

Garmston and Wellman (2016) refer to *norms* as the skills the team works on until they become "normal behavior in the group." They explain that "When this occurs, the behavior becomes normative for new group members, who model their own behavior on the standards tacitly set by group veterans" (p. 42). When operational norms are clear, observable, and measurable, we can hold ourselves and one another accountable, while also noting and celebrating when each norm positively effects the PLC+ effort.

Sometimes, there will already be schoolwide operating norms that have been developed for all PLC+ teams. If this is the case, then we recommend that your team should utilize these norms—with the following caveat. Ask yourself: *Are these norms rooted in the **why** behind the PLC+?* If you've inherited norms that you're planning to use, it is important for the PLC+ team to discuss them and make any necessary revisions before adopting them as your own.

The following steps will help you develop norms from scratch. If you have already drafted a set of norms, consider using them for Step 1.

Approach	How to Activate
Generate Norms (5 minutes)	Distribute a set of index cards and markers to each PLC+ team member. Ask each team member to write down *one* group norm they would like to see, using only one side of the card and omitting their name. Members should not include more than one norm per card but may write as many cards as they would like.
Review and Group (20 minutes)	Designate a materials manager. Then gather all the cards, shuffle them, and randomly redistribute them to team members. Ask a participant to read out loud the cards they have been given, and then ask other team members to share any cards that are the same or closely related to the one that was just read. After each card is read, the materials manager should collect them and post them in groups that are similar (e.g., "respect," "disagreements," "agenda," etc.). Limit the discussion to grouping norms and identifying similarities between norms.
Dissent Option (5 minutes)	After the materials manager arranges all cards into categories (though some will stand alone), any team member can propose to eliminate any norm. If one other participant seconds a proposal to eliminate a particular norm, then the index card of that norm should be removed.
Condense and Consolidate (30 minutes)	The team discusses condensing each group of norms into a single norm (without stringing them all together with the use of *and*). The goal is to create a single norm that captures the essence of the group of like ideas.
Next Steps	The final product is a list of four to six group norms that will govern all discourse among the team. Record the agreed-upon norms and review the group norms at the beginning of every team meeting.

Source: Adapted from Venables, D. R. (2011). *The practice of authentic PLCs: A guide to effective teacher teams*. Corwin.

SUCCESS CHECKLIST

✓	Activation Task
	Note Potential Challenges
☐	Meetings frequently go off topic or lack structure.
☐	Disengagement, uneven participation, and/or recurring conflict exists among team members.
☐	There is a lack of clarity around expectations for collaboration and communication.
	Activate
☐	Facilitate a team discussion to collaboratively develop or refine clear, measurable norms.
☐	Incorporate norm-setting protocols, such as card sorting and consensus building.
☐	Revisit established norms regularly and use them to guide meeting structure and team accountability.
	Reflect and Refine
☐	How do the team's current norms support or hinder productive collaboration?
☐	What behaviors or patterns signal that the team's norms need to be revisited?
☐	How can the group ensure that new team members adopt and contribute to the team norms?

Notes

_____
_____
_____
_____
_____
_____
_____
_____
_____
_____
_____
_____

29. MEETING MOVES: ESTABLISHING PLC+ ROLES

What are the typical PLC+ roles, and how do we assign roles in a way that best supports the PLC+ effort?					
When					
	Before Meetings	✓	During Meetings		After Meetings
How Often					
✓	Planning		Implementation		Reflection

STRATEGY-AT-A-GLANCE

There are defined roles and responsibilities within a PLC+ that, together, support the success of your team effort. Becoming aware of the roles, as well as making strategic assignments based on team member expertise and ability, will help accelerate your team's performance and impact.

RECOGNIZING THE NEED

At Maplewood Middle School, a group of teachers eagerly forms a team to improve student outcomes. However, without defined roles, their meetings quickly become unproductive. Discussions spiral in circles, with no one keeping notes or ensuring follow-ups. Mrs. Patel, a veteran teacher, tries to lead, but others hesitate, unsure if she has the authority. Mr. Gomez, skilled in data analysis, assumes everyone will track student progress, but no one does. Ms. Carter, the most organized among them, grows frustrated that tasks are forgotten, and weeks pass without any real progress. Eventually recognizing their situation, they finally establish clear roles: an activator to guide discussions, a recorder to track action steps, and a data analyst to monitor student performance. With structure in place, meetings become focused, collaboration improves, and ideas turn into action.

ACTIVATING WITH THIS STRATEGY

The result of your PLC+ team's work in *Your Introduction to PLC+* prepares you and your colleagues for the natural establishment of roles. Members are most likely to take action by stepping into roles that align with the strengths of the PLC+ once they have accomplished the following:

- Zeroed in on the four crosscutting values
- Gained a deep understanding of the PLC+ framework
- Viewed the outcomes as significant for teaching and learning
- Recognized and acknowledged the strengths they bring to the PLC+ team

Levi (2014), who suggested that roles are one of the "basic building blocks" of a team's success, also noted that successful teams are able to describe the roles and responsibilities of an effective group and explain how each role relates to what others in the group are doing (p. 69). Division of labor should also require individual ownership of specific duties, which can also engage team members. Allowing them to work in their areas of strength as they work for the good of the whole creates positive interdependence. Remember that teammates can be assigned multiple roles within the PLC+ framework.

The following table presents a brief description of a set of aligned qualities for the important roles PLC+ team members can assume.

Role	Description	Recommended Qualities
Team Activator (likely, YOU)	Keeps the team focused on the foundational pieces of the PLC+ process and consistently moves the learning of the group forward	Has strong collaboration skills Is trusted and respected by team members Is knowledgeable about effective, research-based instructional practices
Engaged Participant(s)	(Note Potential Challenges: This role applies to *everyone* on the team. Meeting success is based much more on the informed participation and input of PLC+ team members than on one person in authority, an expert, or an appointed leader [Garmston, 2012, p. 28]) Comes prepared and on time to meetings Knows their strengths and weaknesses as a contributor and activator Stays focused on the meeting's specific tasks and on the PLC+'s overarching purposes Listens and responds carefully to others Contributes respectfully and with the motive of moving the team forward	Is able to focus attention on the immediate agenda, topics, challenges, and opportunities—and eliminate unnecessary distractions for the time being
Note-Taker	Keeps a record of the important information generated by the PLC+ meetings Coordinates communication of minutes to all stakeholders within agreed-upon and realistic time frame Sends agenda and any pertinent information to stakeholders to read or understand prior to the meeting	Is an organized summarizer Meets deadlines Has effective writing and communication skills

(Continued)

(Continued)

Role	Description	Recommended Qualities
Data Technician	Activates the charting of data and other evidence Compiles data from PLC+ team into a usable format prior to meetings Creates and develops charts, graphs, spreadsheets, and other representations of data and evidence	Is organized Enjoys working with data Can effectively use Excel or other data software Is able to condense student evidence and data into usable charts and graphs
Instructional Researcher	(Note Potential Challenges: This role can be held simultaneously by multiple individuals within the PLC+) Researches effective research-based instructional strategies Provides deeper insights into how strategies can be used and implemented as possible solutions to address students' identified needs related to guiding Question 2 of the PLC+ framework	Is knowledgeable about educational research and effective instructional practice Desires to seek out new strategies to support adult and student learning needs
Timekeeper	Helps PLC+ team stay on track with time frames agreed upon for agenda items, guiding questions, and discussion or decision points Makes sure to utilize an external timer and to set it with an audible alarm to keep agenda moving and ensure that team focus does not get unnecessarily off track However, recognizes when to let the time expire and not stop the productive dialogue that may be occurring at that moment	Is willing to keep team focused on time commitments Is able to decide when to interject—such as when time commitments must be adhered to in order to allow the team to stay on track with time constraints—and when to allow more time than initially planned
Data Wall Curator	Maintains team data displays to communicate the effectiveness of strategies being implemented—aligned with evidence of the impact of these strategies in helping to accelerate student learning Coalesces data and evidence into usable charts and graphs for the PLC+ team and other school stakeholders	Is creative in nature Is willing to devote time to developing displays of student data and evidence for internal PLC+ use and public (schoolwide) use

We have explored the idea of local contexts and the need for adaptations. To fine-tune these roles to best suit your group's needs, share this information with your PLC+. As a group, use a highlighter, marker, and/or sticky notes to adapt the roles to meet the local strengths of your PLC+.

SUCCESS CHECKLIST

✓	Activation Task
	Note Potential Challenges
☐	A lack of defined roles leads to confusion and inefficiency.
☐	Discussions become unproductive because there is no one activating the PLC+.
☐	Team members hesitate to take ownership because there are no clear expectations.
	Activate
☐	Establish clear roles based upon the full range of roles and responsibilities.
☐	Encourage members to step into roles that align with their strengths.
☐	Regularly review and adjust roles to enhance team effectiveness.
	Reflect and Refine
☐	How well-defined are the team roles, and do they support the team's goals?
☐	Are the PLC+ meetings productive, and do they lead to actionable outcomes?
☐	Do all members feel empowered to contribute effectively?

Notes

30. MEETING MOVES: FINDING SOLID GROUND IN ASSESSMENTS AND DATA

How can I use assessments and data to center the PLC+ team?					
When					
	Before Meetings	✓	During Meetings		After Meetings
How Often					
	Planning	✓	Implementation		Reflection

Strategy in Action | Finding Solid Ground in Assessments and Data

qrs.ly/8dgpghf

STRATEGY-AT-A-GLANCE

Assessment data are critical to any PLC+ effort. The regular infusion of data—and reflection on its meaning—helps push the team forward while also informing continuous improvement. Deeply understanding the full range of assessments, engaging in professional learning around assessment, and making wise investments of time to engage with assessment are all positive ways to support any PLC+ effort.

RECOGNIZING THE NEED

Ms. Howser comments, "Some teachers simply don't have any faith in the assessments, or they act like they don't. I hear comments about how we are better than any assessment can measure, or how the tests are just for the state." Whether these comments and the skepticism embedded in them constitute a genuine concern or a defense mechanism, suggestions to not make use of the available evidence and data can bring most conversations about teaching and learning to a screeching halt. Ms. Howser decides to use several approaches that work to turn the skepticism around assessments and data into productive dialogue.

ACTIVATING WITH THIS STRATEGY

PLC+ efforts require teachers to review evidence, or data, about their teaching and learning. Sometimes these data point to strengths and accomplishments—in essence, the kinds of happy endings many of us entered the profession to experience. As well, the data often bring to light opportunities for improvement to teaching and learning that benefits teachers and student alike. But what happens if team members raise skepticism about an assessment and the data it returns?

When such skepticism exists, it can act as a barrier, preventing team members from using the available data to encourage dialogue about two important questions: How do we move learning forward? Who did and did not benefit from our teaching? To help the PLC+ team find solid ground in assessments and data, consider these suggestions.

Approach	How to Activate
Assessments *of*, *for*, and *as* Learning	Teams should compare and contrast the different relationships between assessments and learning. When team members are aware that an assessment can be used *as* learning and *for* learning, this awareness can help ease their defensiveness. This is especially true in cases where team members have seen only assessments as assessments *of* learning—and, thus, of their instruction—rather than the bigger picture that encompasses assessments *for* and *as* learning.
Professional Development	Take note when the team's understanding of "assessment *of*, *for*, and *as* learning" presents with misconceptions. In these cases, the PLC+ should consider professional learning about formative and summative assessments, how to interpret assessment data, and how to use those data to make decisions.
Time Management	PLC+ teams can look for ways to assess student learning without reducing instructional time. For example, investigate the amount of time currently devoted to assessments, then consider how to reduce that time by making assessment part of instruction.
Student Voice and Perspective	Invite students to reflect on and discuss their own assessment experiences and bring their reflections to your PLC+ dialog. Understanding how students perceive assessments can shift teacher mindsets and promote more student-centered data use.
Data Triangulation	Encourage the use of multiple sources of data (e.g., student work samples, classroom observations, and formal assessments) to build a fuller, more accurate picture of learning and progress.

SUCCESS CHECKLIST

✓	Activation Task
	Note Potential Challenges
☐	There is skepticism about assessments—or defensiveness when discussing assessment results—among the PLC+ team.
☐	There are misconceptions about assessment types and purposes.
☐	There are concerns about excessive time spent on assessments.
	Activate
☐	Use PLC+ conversations to clarify different types of assessments.
☐	Engage in professional development on formative and summative assessments.
☐	Facilitate discussions to address concerns and build trust in data.
	Reflect and Refine
☐	How do assessments support or hinder student learning?
☐	Are the team's beliefs about assessments affecting their willingness to use data?
☐	What additional steps can the team take to foster a data-informed culture in the PLC+?

Notes

31. MEETING MOVES: SOCIAL EMOTIONAL CHECK-INS

	\multicolumn{6}{c}{How do I create space for emotional check-ins that strengthen trust, support well-being, and improve collaboration within my PLC+ team?}

	\multicolumn{5}{c}{When}
	Before Meetings	✓	During Meetings		After Meetings
	\multicolumn{5}{c}{How Often}
	Planning	✓	Implementation		Reflection

STRATEGY-AT-A-GLANCE

Social-emotional check-ins create a space for educators to acknowledge their emotional state, reset, and prepare to engage meaningfully in collaborative work. This strategy promotes trust, empathy, and connection within PLC+ teams, leading to more productive and focused meetings. Regular check-ins also help teams identify unseen barriers and build psychological safety, increasing collective efficacy over time. Embedding a brief, structured check-in at the beginning of meetings supports emotional well-being while fostering a culture of compassion and professionalism. Benefits can include reduced stress, stronger relationships, greater innovation, and sustained engagement with the PLC+ work. When people feel seen and supported, they do their best thinking—and their best collaborating.

RECOGNIZING THE NEED

On a rainy Thursday morning, the energy in Room 12 is heavy. "I've had three parent emails and a tech issue before nine a.m.," groans Mr. Leary, barely looking up from his laptop.

Ms. Chen offers a sympathetic smile, and the activator, Ms. Gaines, gently interrupts any further conversation, saying, "Before we dive in—how about we pause, check in, and see where everyone's at?"

That five-minute reset transforms the room, turning scattered stress into shared focus and reigniting their sense of purpose.

ACTIVATING WITH THIS STRATEGY

Begin by establishing a norm for brief emotional check-ins at the start of each PLC+ meeting. This creates a rhythm and an expectation that personal well-being matters and is respected by the team. Check-ins may be formal (using structured questions) or informal (simple go-arounds or open reflections). Consistency builds comfort and trust.

Here is a structured model that includes four rotating questions designed to guide your PLC+ team's check-ins. Each participant answers and then invites the next PLC+ member to join in, ensuring every voice is heard.

Questions	Benefits
How are you feeling today?	The process helps team members
Do you need a check-in after the meeting?	• Center themselves
What is your goal for today's meeting?	• Surface unspoken needs
Who can help you with that?	• Align goals for the session

For activators, check-ins offer a valuable pulse on team morale. They may reveal emotional states that could affect collaboration or signal a need to reframe the agenda. When team members express challenges, offer support or flexibility as needed.

SUCCESS CHECKLIST

✓	Activation Task
	Note Potential Challenges
☐	Emotional tension or stress affects team engagement or productivity.
☐	Individuals are consistently quiet or withdrawn during meetings.
☐	There is inconsistent participation or unclear individual goals during sessions.
	Activate
☐	Introduce and model a consistent social-emotional check-in routine at the start of every meeting.
☐	Use guiding questions to help team members express needs, set goals, and offer support.
☐	Adjust meeting tone or agenda based on team emotional needs as identified in the check-in.
	Reflect and Refine
☐	How are emotional check-ins influencing the quality of the team's collaboration?
☐	Are all team members feeling safe and supported enough to share openly?
☐	What can you do as an activator to model empathy and foster emotional trust?

32. MEETING MOVES: UTILIZING AUTHENTIC INSTRUCTIONAL PROTOCOLS

> How do I guide my PLC+ team to select and use instructional protocols with purpose, aligning them to our goals, guiding questions, and collaborative needs for deeper impact?

When					
	Before Meetings	✓	During Meetings		After Meetings
How Often					
	Planning	✓	Implementation		Reflection

STRATEGY-AT-A-GLANCE

Authentic instructional protocols provide structure and depth to PLC+ collaboration. When carefully selected and purposefully timed, these protocols elevate teacher dialogue, reflection, and practice. Strategic use of the book *Your Introduction to PLC+* ensures alignment with team goals, guiding questions, and shared values.

RECOGNIZING THE NEED

"This protocol feels like another checkbox." Mr. Jordan sighs as he skims the task sheet.

Ms. Wu nods and says, "We keep using tools, but I'm not sure we've ever really talked about why we're using them."

Ms. De La Cruz, their activator, leans in and says, "Let's back up and ask: What are we trying to shift in our practice—and what's the best tool to help us do that?"

With that, the team begins a new approach—choosing protocols not by routine, but by purpose.

ACTIVATING WITH THIS STRATEGY

Authentic instructional protocols are most effective when they are selected intentionally based on the team's goals, focus questions, and collaborative maturity. Rather than completing every task or worksheet in *Your Introduction to PLC+*, activators guide teams to identify the right entry point and choose tools that align with their *why* and *how*.

To begin, activators should lead a professional learning experience in which team members become familiar with the modules associated with the five guiding questions. Use a cooperative learning strategy to engage team members in exploring which protocols best serve the team's current needs, goals, and context.

The process should be collaborative. Seek input from all members and be responsive to their experiences and insights. Teams should explore which activities or tasks within the modules will support instructional reflection and effective learning strategies for students.

Finally, be flexible and thoughtful in timing. Some protocols are time intensive and may be best suited for early-cycle deep dives, while others support midcycle adjustments or reflection points. By intentionally using protocols when they're most impactful, PLC+ teams foster stronger alignment, more meaningful collaboration, and greater instructional effectiveness.

Approach	How to Activate
Purpose-Driven Protocol Selection	Choose instructional protocols based on the team's current goals, guiding questions, and level of collaborative maturity. Focus on alignment with the team's *why* and *how*.
Professional Learning on Modules	Lead a session to help team members explore *Your Introduction to PLC+* modules associated with the five guiding questions. Build understanding before implementation.
Collaborative Decision Making	Engage all team members in identifying which protocols are most relevant. Use cooperative structures to ensure input and ownership across the team.
Timing and Responsiveness	Be flexible in protocol use. Select time-intensive protocols for deep dives early in the cycle and use shorter, targeted protocols midcycle to support refinement.
Ongoing Reflection and Adjustment	Regularly review how protocols are supporting team and student learning. Adjust selections based on feedback and observed impact.

SUCCESS CHECKLIST

✓	Activation Task
	Note Potential Challenges
☐	Protocols are being used routinely without clear connection to the PLC+ question or team goal.
☐	There is a lack of team understanding about the purpose or process of the instructional protocol.
☐	There is resistance or disengagement from team members during protocol use.
	Activate
☐	Facilitate a professional learning session to build understanding of the *Your Introduction to PLC+* modules and protocols.
☐	Collaboratively choose protocols that align with team goals, needs, and phases of the inquiry cycle.
☐	Adjust the timing and selection of protocols to best support collaboration and effectiveness throughout the cycle.
	Reflect and Refine
☐	Is the team using instructional protocols that align with the PLC+ focus and goals?
☐	How are these protocols improving the quality of the team's dialogue and instructional decisions?
☐	What changes could make the team's protocol use more effective or engaging?

Notes

_____
_____
_____
_____
_____
_____
_____
_____
_____
_____

Norms of Collaborative Work

An Introduction to Norms of Collaborative Work

qrs.ly/sqgpghl

33. NORMS OF COLLABORATIVE WORK 1: PAUSING

How do we create conversational spaces during meetings so ideas and insights can emerge?					
When					
	Before Meetings	✓	During Meetings		After Meetings
How Often					
	Planning	✓	Implementation		Reflection

STRATEGY-AT-A-GLANCE

To deepen the social cohesion of the group, members need to utilize communication tools that signal active listening and the supportive exchanges of ideas. The seven norms of collaborative work from cognitive coaching are useful for developing communication skills that address the relational elements essential to deep collaboration (Costa & Garmston, 2015).

The first of these is pausing. The rush to solve problems and quickly take action can thwart a team's potential to positively impact student and adult learning. Deliberate attention to pausing in conversations allows for all members to contemplate and consider their ideas and those of others.

RECOGNIZING THE NEED

A small team of educators at Hilltop Middle School have identified their common challenge: *Students find it difficult to sustain extended academic discussions.* Ironically, what has quickly become apparent is that the team itself is also having trouble sustaining their own discussions. Two members seem to be carrying most of the conversation, with little input from others. Raheem Jackson, an activator on the team, has noticed that the lack of participation by others may not be due to a lack of interest, but rather few spaces in the group's dialogue for other perspectives to take root.

ACTIVATING WITH THIS STRATEGY

Although this step is deceptively simple, pausing provides opportunities for speakers to extend their thinking and for listeners to consider what has been said. The opposite of speaking is not waiting to speak again—it's listening. Pausing is analogous to the wait-time practices we know are critical to foster student discourse. Wait time is used in classrooms because it has been reliably shown to encourage longer student responses and more critical thinking (Wasik & Hindman, 2018). Purposeful pausing allows time for the listeners to process what has been said before attempting to share additional information. Pausing gives the speakers time to consider their own ideas. It also signals to the speakers and the listeners that contributions are valued.

Approach	How to Activate
Highlight pausing as a communication tool.	Connect educators' prior knowledge of the usefulness of Wait Time 1 (after a question has been asked) and Wait Time 2 (after a response is given) to elicit student thinking.
Model pausing in your own communication.	<ul><li>Refrain from speaking over others.</li><li>Allow time when the speaker finishes before adding information.</li><li>Actively listen when others are speaking.</li></ul>
Schedule collective Pause breaks during team discussions.	The team is making important decisions. Schedule Pause breaks in the agenda that correspond with decisions about actions.
Listen for opportunities to take unscheduled pauses.	<ul><li>Pause after someone has shared a positive story related to the team's work.</li><li>Pause after a troubling or disquieting story related to the team's work has been shared.</li></ul>

SUCCESS CHECKLIST

✓	Activation Task
	Note Potential Challenges
☐	There is a lack of verbal participation by some members.
☐	Talking over one another is routine.
☐	Decisions are hurried and not fully formed.
	Activate
☐	Model pausing and active listening in your own communication.
☐	Schedule pauses in your agenda that correspond to key decision points.
☐	When appropriate, schedule written pauses of one or two minutes to elicit new thinking.
	Reflect and Refine
☐	Where does the team tend to pause during the PLC+ conversations or meetings?
☐	How comfortable is the team with silence during the discussions?
☐	Is the team seeing increased participation in consequential decision making as a result of the efforts to pause and allow thinking time?

Notes

_____
_____
_____
_____
_____
_____
_____
_____
_____
_____
_____
_____
_____
_____

34. NORMS OF COLLABORATIVE WORK 2: PARAPHRASING

Do we have processes for clarifying understanding when we are confused?					
When					
	Before Meetings	✔	During Meetings		After Meetings
How Often					
	Planning	✔	Implementation		Reflection

Strategy in Action | Paraphrasing

qrs.ly/8ugpghm

STRATEGY-AT-A-GLANCE

Paraphrasing in group communication is the act of restating another person's message in your own words to confirm understanding. It shows active listening, helps clarify meaning, and ensures that everyone is aligned in the conversation. By paraphrasing, team members can reduce misunderstandings and create a more collaborative and respectful dialogue. Paraphrasing confers the group's respect and confirms the value of the speaker who hears the emotional subtext: "We are striving to understand you."

RECOGNIZING THE NEED

The upper-elementary-grades team at Elm Elementary has identified a common challenge related to reading comprehension of informational texts but is disagreeing on next steps. First-year teacher Helen Cammarata expresses concern about the timeline: The state assessments are scheduled for the next quarter, and she is concerned about her students with Individualized Education Programs (IEPs). Fourth-grade special educator Melissa Hunter responds defensively, assuming the concern is a criticism of her work supporting students in general education classrooms. The team is growing uncomfortable and needs to deescalate the tension, clarify intent, and refocus on problem solving.

ACTIVATING WITH THIS STRATEGY

Costa and Garmston (2015) note that paraphrasing is an underutilized communication tool. Yet paraphrasing has the potential to move the group's thinking forward. The speaker's statements are recast to ensure that what has been understood is accurate and complete. However, there is an intentional avoidance of "I-statements," as they can shift the focus from paraphrasing the speaker's remarks to the person doing the paraphrasing.

Approach	How to Activate
Use acknowledging statements.	"You're concerned about . . ." "You're wondering if . . ." "Let me try to put that in my own words." "Let me reflect back what I think you meant . . ." "It sounds like you're trying to help us avoid a pitfall—do I have that right?"
Organize the member's statement.	"If I'm hearing you right, you're saying . . ." "So, there are four things you're concerned about." "On the one hand _____, and on the other hand _____." Note Potential Challenges: This paraphrasing technique is especially useful when speakers are recounting experiences that they have not yet fully processed.
Attempt to elevate the speaker's thinking from an anecdote to a larger but perhaps unstated issue.	"So, a goal of yours is . . ." "You value . . ." "It is important to you that . . ."

SUCCESS CHECKLIST

✓	Activation Task
	Note Potential Challenges
☐	PLC+ team members are talking past each other or repeating their points without acknowledgment.
☐	Phrases or tones often suggest that clarification or deeper understanding is needed (e.g., "Wait, I thought you were saying . . .")
☐	Side conversations indicate that people are struggling to process what has been stated.
	Activate
☐	Recenter the conversation. "Let me see if I can pull us back. It sounds like what we're really trying to figure out is . . ." "So to bring us back to the main point, are we saying that . . ."
☐	Surface unspoken assumptions or interpretations. "It sounds like there's an underlying concern about trust or accountability—does that feel accurate?" "Just to check—are we assuming that this approach won't work based on past experiences?"
☐	Reduce defensiveness by clarifying intent. "I think what you're trying to say is that the concern is with the system, not the person—does that capture it?" "Just to clarify: You're not criticizing the effort, but pointing out a pattern that's been frustrating—right?"
	Reflect and Refine
☐	How often do team members clarify someone's meaning by putting it into their own words?
☐	When someone shares an idea, do team members pause to reflect it back—or do they jump straight to responding or debating?
☐	Are there times when paraphrasing could have prevented miscommunication or frustration?

35. NORMS OF COLLABORATIVE WORK 3: POSING QUESTIONS

How do we ensure that we are taking the time to consider multiple perspectives and interrogate our assumptions?					
When					
	Before Meetings	✓	During Meetings		After Meetings
How Often					
	Planning	✓	Implementation		Reflection

Strategy in Action | Posing Questions

qrs.ly/1hgpgho

STRATEGY-AT-A-GLANCE

Once the team has reached an initial understanding, members can pose questions. The first questions should further clarify the details and be factual and closed in nature, such as, *"How many students were in the group?"* Once necessary details have been covered, open-ended probes should be utilized. Open-ended questions are inquiries that invite elaboration, reflection, or explanation rather than a simple yes-or-no answer. They encourage deeper thinking and richer conversation by allowing the responder to share ideas, perspectives, or experiences in their own words.

RECOGNIZING THE NEED

Sheila McCormick has been designated as the note-taker for her PLC+ team meetings and takes her job seriously, However, in an effort to capture the discussion, she is peppering the team with lots of closed questions that are focused narrowly on details. The team is growing restless, as they seem to want to dive in more deeply to explore the nuances that are emerging.

ACTIVATING WITH THIS STRATEGY

Costa and Garmston (2015) caution that our posed questions should not be thinly veiled suggestions (e.g., "Have you ever considered using a graphic organizer?"). Rather, the intention is to mediate the speaker's thinking. One of our favorite prompts from the cognitive coaching framework is to ask, *"What are your hunches about _____?"* and then let the person talk. You'll know that your probing questions are doing the job when you hear speakers respond with their own reflective insights. Taken together, pausing, paraphrasing, and posing questions compose a cycle of norms put into action. Far more than the norm "listen as an ally," these three techniques convey that members are valued, listened to without judgment, and seen as people as well as educators.

50 Strategies for Activating Your PLC+

Approach	How to Activate
Allow for multiple valid answers that foster diverse thinking, not just one solution.	*"What might be some different ways to approach this common challenge, besides the two we have discussed?"* *"Before we move forward, what haven't we considered yet?"*
Shift from the specific to the systemic.	*"Do we think this might be part of a larger pattern?"* *"What does this example reveal about the bigger picture?"* *"Is this situation connected to something we've seen before?"*
Explore underlying beliefs or structures.	*"What might this say about our norms or assumptions?"* *"Could this be pointing to an issue with our current process or system?"* *"Is there a deeper concern here that we haven't named yet?"*
Invite broader reflection.	*"What might others be experiencing in similar situations?"* *"If this keeps happening, what might that tell us about our culture or expectations?"* *"How might this one story help us understand the common challenge?"*

SUCCESS CHECKLIST

✓	Activation Task
	Note Potential Challenges
☐	Only one or two people are dominating the discussion.
☐	Team members are nodding along without real cognitive engagement.
☐	The discussion seems to be moving too quickly toward a solution without exploring options.
	Activate
☐	Pose questions that are curious, not leading (e.g., "What are the implications of this decision for different stakeholders?").
☐	Pose questions that invite reflection, not reaction. They give space for processing, rather than pushing for quick opinions (e.g., "What assumptions might we be making without realizing it?").
☐	Focus on impact (e.g., "How does this connect to our core purpose or values?").
	Reflect and Refine
☐	How often do team members use open-ended questions to deepen the understanding of an issue?
☐	Do team members' questions invite multiple perspectives and encourage reflection—or do they close down thinking?
☐	When the team feels stuck, does the group use open-ended questions to help reframe the problem?

Notes

36. NORMS OF COLLABORATIVE WORK 4: PROVIDING DATA

How do we discuss our qualitative and quantitative data to make decisions?					
When					
	Before Meetings	✓	During Meetings		After Meetings
How Often					
	Planning	✓	Implementation		Reflection

STRATEGY-AT-A-GLANCE

Providing data is an essential practice for professional learning communities. This includes quantitative data, such as test scores, as well as qualitative data garnered from exit slips, interviews, observations, emails from families, and surveys. How the data are discussed—and the courage the team must sit with the data—can transform the team's impact from resignation to resolve.

RECOGNIZING THE NEED

Union High School's mathematics PLC+ is feeling defeated. The eleventh-grade state test scores from last spring were below expectations. "I thought we did so many things last year, but the results don't show it," says George Pham.

His colleague Desiree Milton echoes the same sentiment. "I'm not sure what else we can do. We looked at the previous year's test scores last fall, and I thought we came up with a really good plan. I really don't know why we bother. We could better use this time to get our lesson plans and grading done."

ACTIVATING WITH THIS STRATEGY

There are three elements that are essential to data discussion. The first is to depersonalize the data. Rather than frame it as "your third-period results" or "our intervention program," try using depersonalized language: "the results" or "the program." It's human nature to feel defensive when data you are involved with are negative. Nonjudgmental and depersonalized data discussions build a sense of safety and trust in the group.

The second element in a data discussion is striving to find the story behind the data. This is especially important when the data are quantitative, as the numbers can eclipse the humans they represent and the context in which they were gathered.

The third element of data collection is asking what other data might broaden the group's understanding. Be careful that the data are not explained away. It takes courage to stick with the data and act upon them. The team's willingness to sit with the data, consider possibilities, and seek to understand the underlying story signal a caring but resolute disposition.

Approach	How to Activate
Start with curiosity, not judgment.	Ask *"What story is the data telling us?"* rather than *"What's going wrong?"*
Share, don't sell.	A principle of liberatory design is to present data so that others can reach their own conclusions. *"Let's explore what this might mean before jumping to conclusions."* *"What are we noticing? What questions does this raise?"* *"Let's assume positive intent and dig deeper into the patterns."*
Focus on learning, not blaming.	*"Let's separate the data from the people—we're here to learn, not to assign fault."* *"What systems or supports might be influencing these outcomes?"* *"What factors are within our influence?"*
Use open-ended questions to deepen thinking.	*"What do you see in the data that makes you say that?"* *"What are some possible explanations?"* *"What questions does this raise for us as a team?"*
Balance numbers with narratives.	*"What do we know from our experience that gives context to this data?"* *"What might this look or sound like in a classroom?"* *"What do students say about this issue?"*

SUCCESS CHECKLIST

✓	Activation Task
	Note Potential Challenges
☐	The PLC+ team is blaming individuals (e.g., "those kids," "that teacher," "that class") instead of exploring systems.
☐	The team is cherry-picking data or ignoring uncomfortable data by focusing only on the data that support a predetermined narrative.
☐	There is a failure to follow through (e.g., "*That was a great conversation—but let's move on*").
	Activate
☐	Pair quantitative data (test scores, attendance) with student interviews, work samples, or survey data.
☐	Create and use a shared list of open-ended prompts (e.g., "*What patterns do we see?*" "*Whose experience does this reflect?*").
☐	Avoid naming individuals when discussing outcomes. Focus on patterns, not people.
	Reflect and Refine
☐	What is not shown in this data set that the team might need to consider to understand the full picture?
☐	Whose voices or experiences are reflected in this data? Whose are missing?
☐	How might students and families interpret this data differently?

Notes

37. NORMS OF COLLABORATIVE WORK 5: PUTTING IDEAS ON THE TABLE

How do we explore—and refine—ideas so we can make decisions?					
When					
	Before Meetings	✓	During Meetings		After Meetings
How Often					
	Planning	✓	Implementation		Reflection

STRATEGY-AT-A-GLANCE

It's essential that teams feel safe and empowered to put ideas on the table, as this openness fuels innovation, problem solving, and collective efficacy. When team members can share thoughts without fear of judgment, diverse perspectives surface and deeper understanding emerges. Putting ideas on the table and considering their merit is characteristic of high-performing groups (Senge et al., 2012). To interrogate ideas without masking them, use neutral language to separate the idea from the person. Also remember that it's just as important to take ideas off the table when they don't serve the group's purpose or direction (Costa & Garmston, 2015).

RECOGNIZING THE NEED

During their weekly PLC+ meeting, the seventh-grade social studies team sits quietly, the air thick with hesitation. They have been asked to develop solutions for chronic absenteeism at the school, but no one responds right away. A few team members glance at each other, while others avoid eye contact, busying themselves with laptops or notepads. One teacher cautiously suggests a potential outreach strategy, but it's met with silence and a quick pivot back to the agenda. Over time, the group has developed an unspoken norm of keeping ideas close, fearing judgment, pushback, or being seen as too critical. As a result, the team struggles to make progress on persistent challenges, remaining stuck in surface-level discussions and missing opportunities for collaboration.

ACTIVATING WITH THIS STRATEGY

Great teams get better over time at putting ideas on the table (offering them up for consideration) and taking them off the table (letting go of ideas that don't serve the group's purpose or direction). However, there may be hurdles in this area that the group needs to face. For example, if the person who suggests an idea is in a particular role or is a knowledge authority, then the group may be reluctant to challenge the idea because of the source (even when it's not an especially useful idea). Similarly, two members who have a history of conflict between them may not be able to entertain the possibility that the other person's idea is a good one. Conversely, two members who are friends may agree with each other no matter what because they don't want to risk hurt feelings. As another example, a member's ideas may be disregarded because he has the least credibility with his students. Each of these potential situations marks a stage when the wheels can come off the proverbial bus. The team may find itself unable to move forward, or they may move in the wrong direction, because the relationships got in the way.

Approach	How to Activate
Establish psychological safety.	Normalize idea sharing as a learning behavior, not a performance (e.g., "All ideas are welcome here. We're not judging; we're exploring.")
Use neutral language to separate the idea from the person.	"I'm not advocating for this idea. I'm thinking aloud about . . ." "This might not be fully formed, but here's something I'm thinking about . . ." "A possible idea would be . . ." "Would you consider . . . ?" "What if . . . ?"
Make it low risk to contribute.	Use sticky notes, shared documents, or anonymous idea collection when needed. Emphasize exploration over evaluation in early stages.
Take ideas off the table when needed.	When the discussion seems to get stuck in the proverbial cul-de-sac of circular thinking, it may be time to narrow the ideas. This requires naming and releasing ideas respectfully. "It seems like this idea is blocking our thinking. Let's set it aside for now and come back to it again later if we still think it's relevant." "That idea helped us think in a new direction, but it may not serve us best right now."
Create decision-making agreements.	Clarify how decisions are made (consensus, majority, recommendation). Set norms like this one: "Once we've explored ideas, we'll decide together which ones move forward."
Use criteria to evaluate ideas.	Bring in filters to align with the team's goals, feasibility, and impact. "Which of these ideas best meets our purpose?" "Which ideas feel most actionable?"

(Continued)

(Continued)

Approach	How to Activate
Celebrate the role of all ideas.	Acknowledge that even set-aside ideas had value in the process. *"That idea really helped us think differently."* *"Every contribution moves the group forward, even if we don't use it."* *"Thanks for naming that—it took courage, and it mattered."* Create a "Thinking Wall" or an "Idea Archive" as a visible record of all ideas shared (e.g., chart paper or Google Doc).

SUCCESS CHECKLIST

✓	Activation Task
	Note Potential Challenges
☐	The group is skipping from idea to idea without deeper discussion or analysis.
☐	There is a lack of note-taking or visible tracking of ideas shared.
☐	The team quickly dismisses new ideas (e.g., rolls eyes, laughs, interrupts, moves on without acknowledgment).
	Activate
☐	Define a clear focus or question to prevent ideas from becoming too vague.
☐	Make the thinking visible by writing all ideas down on a board or shared document.
☐	Make decisions to plan next steps. Have a process in place to narrow ideas and move to action.
	Reflect and Refine
☐	What helps team members feel safe to contribute ideas? What gets in the way?
☐	Do team members explain why certain ideas are set aside, or do the ideas just fade without closure?
☐	Are team members striking a good balance between generating ideas and narrowing them down?

38. NORMS OF COLLABORATIVE WORK 6: PAYING ATTENTION TO SELF AND OTHERS

How do we monitor our own emotions and those of others?					
When					
	Before Meetings	✓	During Meetings		After Meetings
How Often					
	Planning	✓	Implementation		Reflection

STRATEGY-AT-A-GLANCE

Pay attention to your own reactions to ideas and the people who share them, noticing when personal biases may surface. Observe nonverbal cues—your own and others'—to help foster a sense of connection and social cohesion in the group. Stay attuned to the behaviors and actions of others to better understand their emotional state or level of engagement. This awareness can help build trust and improve the quality of collaboration.

RECOGNIZING THE NEED

The tenth-grade team at Desert Bloom High School is multigenerational, with members representing baby boomers, Gen X, millennials, and Gen Z. Although they generally get along, they face a lot of difficulty when it comes to making decisions and taking action in their PLC. Older members are perceived by others as being bossy and controlling; the newest members are variously seen as being either needy or detached. When it comes to communicating effectively to make decisions, the nonverbal messages are pretty divisive.

ACTIVATING WITH THIS STRATEGY

Our mood can bias how we perceive, attend to, interpret, and cognitively organize the ideas being discussed (Bandura, 1997). The intent isn't to remove these mood states—that would be impossible. As humans, we continually process the world through our own specific emotional states. But emotional states are not necessarily the same for everyone in the room. Therefore, it is wise to attend to our own emotions and the signals others use to let us know what theirs are.

Social sensitivity is the ability to perceive and understand the feelings of others. Social cohesion—the glue that binds us together—is a product in part of the social sensitivity of the members of a group or an organization. Be mindful not only of what you say, but also how the message appears to be received by others. Their posture, facial expressions, position, movement, gestures, and eye contact speak volumes that convey far more information than words alone. It is useful to maintain curiosity about the emotional states of others while resisting the urge to react defensively. *"I felt a shift in the mood when I proposed that idea,"* you might say. *"Help me understand the reaction."*

Your own mood is also important. Take an inventory of your impressions as you consider ideas. Did you notice yourself tense up when a particular suggestion was made by another member? If so, don't judge yourself, but instead ask yourself what might be lurking behind the reaction. Perhaps a previous experience did not go well for you, and now you are struggling to reconcile the past with a possible future action. If you need to, ask the group to help you process the experience to understand it better. The first three communication tools—pause, paraphrase, and pose questions—will assist you and the team with working through what might otherwise be an obstacle to action.

Approach	How to Activate
Start meetings with an emotional check-in.	Team meetings are often scheduled just before, during, or right after the school day, meaning that people are often rushing from one event to another. Begin meetings with a quick prompt to normalize emotional presence and give insight into team energy. *"What's one word to describe how you're arriving today?"* *"What's one thing on your mind right now?"*
Use norms to support awareness.	*"Notice your reactions—pause before responding."* *"Pay attention to what's said and unsaid."*
Name what you notice, gently.	Model emotionally intelligent language that conveys curiosity, not judgment. *"I'm sensing some tension—should we pause and check in?"* *"I noticed some silence after that idea. Should we revisit it?"*
Reflect in real time or after the meeting.	Use short writing or team reflection moments: *"What was I feeling in that moment?"* *"How did that impact my contributions?"* *"How did my emotions affect others?"*

SUCCESS CHECKLIST

✓	Activation Task
	Note Potential Challenges
☐	There are few signs of engagement and participation (e.g., people leaning in, taking notes, looking interested).
☐	The emotional tone is negative (e.g., anxious, uncomfortable, lacking excitement, indicating disagreement).
☐	The activator experiences physical cues that are early warning signs of stress and reactivity (e.g., a tight jaw, shallow breathing, and clenched fists).
	Activate
☐	Set the intention. As a team, agree that emotional awareness is part of your collaborative work.
☐	Practice self-awareness during meetings by scheduling a quiet pause midmeeting to reflect without interruption.
☐	Observe others with curiosity, not assumption. Look for nonverbal cues—facial expressions, body language, silence, tone shifts. Ask yourself, *"What might that person be feeling right now?"*
	Reflect and Refine
☐	How did you show up in today's meeting—mentally, emotionally, and energetically?
☐	What verbal and nonverbal emotional cues did you notice in others today?
☐	Were there moments in today's meeting when the team avoided emotions or tension instead of addressing them?

Notes

_____
_____
_____
_____
_____
_____
_____
_____
_____
_____

39. NORMS OF COLLABORATIVE WORK 7: PRESUMING POSITIVE INTENTIONS

How do we reframe when disagreement emerges?					
When					
	Before Meetings	✓	During Meetings		After Meetings
How Often					
	Planning	✓	Implementation		Reflection

Strategy in Action | Presuming Positive Intentions

qrs.ly/46gpghp

STRATEGY-AT-A-GLANCE

Reframing is a vital team communication skill because it helps transform potentially negative or tense moments into opportunities for understanding and growth. By restating a comment, concern, or idea in a more constructive or generous light, professional learning community members make the practice of presuming positive intentions actionable and visible. Reframing doesn't ignore conflict—it redirects it by inviting curiosity, reducing defensiveness, and encouraging collaboration. In doing so, it creates space for dialogue instead of division, helping teams stay focused on shared goals and mutual respect.

RECOGNIZING THE NEED

During a team meeting to work toward the common challenge of developing students' public-speaking skills, fourth-grade teacher Maria Rodriguez suggests shifting the unit to include more student-led extemporaneous presentations. Almost immediately, colleague Kevin Martin responds with a flat tone, saying, "We've already tried that and it didn't go well."

Maria quietly nods and doesn't speak again for the rest of the meeting. No one addresses the exchange, but the energy shifts—people become more reserved, and ideas slow down. Although the moment isn't overtly hostile, the team misses an opportunity to explore the idea further, largely because Kevin has assumed Maria wasn't aware of past challenges, and others have assumed the disagreement isn't worth revisiting.

ACTIVATING WITH THIS STRATEGY

The act of presuming positive intentions could be first, last, and everything in between. It is a tool and also a disposition, and it requires action to sustain it (Costa & Garmston, 2015). But too often the intent appears on the list for a group at the beginning of the school year, only to be quickly forgotten. Although open confrontation is rare, the more common response to it is that members refrain from sharing ideas, thus stunting the agency of the group.

Please recognize that your colleagues are doing the best they know how, as are you. It is rare that any educator wakes up in the morning and thinks, *"I choose to ruin Scott's day today."* (By the way, students don't do this, either.) And yet it happens. Recognize that there are times when we mar someone else's day.

Reframe statements such that they convey a presumption of positive intentions. Saying, *"Our writing scores went down despite our efforts last quarter; what's wrong?"* puts everyone on the defensive, and the blame game begins. In an attempt to deflect, team members may blame the assessment, the curriculum, the students, the two snow days that occurred last month—anything to redirect it away from themselves. Alternatively, in an attempt to maintain the social cohesion, there might be a member who takes the hit for the team: "I didn't do a good job. That's probably why the scores went down." Mind you, there are no data to support that statement, just a desperate need to break the tension.

A reframed statement might be, *"We've got a shared commitment to increasing our students' writing skills. There's lots of things we did last quarter to do so. But the data suggest that we didn't accomplish what we intended. Let's take a closer look at what we think might be contributing to the gap between what we want and where we're at right now."*

Approach	How to Activate
Acknowledge contributions with gratitude.	Respond to ideas with appreciation, even if you disagree. *"Thanks for bringing that up—it's helping us think."* *"I hadn't considered that perspective."*
Pause and notice the initial interpretation.	Encourage team members to become aware of their first reaction. *"Let's consider what stories we are telling ourselves about this."* *"Is there another way to see this?"*
Ask reframing questions.	*"What else might be true?"* *"How might we interpret this differently if we assumed positive intent?"* *"What's another possible explanation for what happened?"*
Share reframes aloud.	*"At first I felt dismissed, but now I'm wondering if the concern came from a place of care."* *"Let me reframe that—I think what we're actually struggling with is uncertainty, not disagreement."*
Translate resistance into insight.	*"That sounds like a really helpful caution—how can we use it to strengthen the plan?"* *"You're pointing out something we need to consider. Let's unpack that."*

SUCCESS CHECKLIST

✓	Activation Task
Note Potential Challenges	
☐	There are negative shifts in the team's energy, such as discomfort after someone speaks (e.g., side glances, shifting in chairs, crossed arms) or a visible split in the group.
☐	The disagreements feel personal (e.g., "you always" or "you never").
☐	The PLC+ team members close notebooks, close laptops, and show other signs of packing up.
Activate	
☐	Ask clarifying questions before assuming meaning.
☐	Use reframing language to reflect professional generosity.
☐	Debrief group dynamics when meetings are tense. "Were there moments where we could have assumed positive intent more actively?"
Reflect and Refine	
☐	What helps you stay open and curious in moments of tension or disagreement?
☐	Are there moments when the team seems to jump to conclusions or assume the worst?
☐	When has the team done well with positive intentions—and what made it possible?

Notes

TEAM DYNAMICS

An Introduction to Team Dynamics
qrs.ly/14gpghq

40. TEAM DYNAMICS: ACHIEVING TEAM PSYCHOLOGICAL SAFETY

How do I create the psychological safety my PLC+ team needs to take risks, speak honestly, and grow together?					
When					
	Before Meetings	✓	During Meetings		After Meetings
How Often					
	Planning	✓	Implementation		Reflection

STRATEGY-AT-A-GLANCE

Intentionally building psychological safety within PLC+ teams supports open dialogue, trust, and continuous improvement. Psychological safety empowers team members to speak up, take risks, and engage authentically—which is crucial for collaborative environments where innovation and learning are key. Grounded in research from Edmondson (2018), this strategy offers a step-by-step approach for leaders and teams to create the conditions that allow every voice to be heard.

RECOGNIZING THE NEED

At Willow Creek Middle School, the seventh-grade PLC+ team is meeting to discuss declining assessment scores. Ms. Alvarez quietly mentions that she's tried a new strategy, but it hasn't worked—but no one responds to acknowledge or support what she's said.

Mr. Bennett suggests redesigning the approach. However, he also worries aloud about the boundaries of his role in the PLC+: "I'm not sure if I'm overstepping."

Ms. Lin, the newest teacher, hesitates before sharing her observations, as if she is fearing judgment. The conversation stalls, and the team realizes that without a foundation of psychological safety, even the best data and plans cannot lead to growth.

ACTIVATING WITH THIS STRATEGY

What do we need, as humans, to feel safe? Psychological safety is the belief that individuals can express themselves without fear of embarrassment, rejection, or punishment. It is not difficult to picture PLC+ team interactions and immediately see the need for this very thing. Timothy Clark's (2020) four stages of psychological safety—Inclusion, Learner, Contributor, and Challenger—are a helpful framework that can guide activators as they work to build trust in stages. Additionally, Amy Edmondson's (2018) work reinforces that psychological safety is especially important in collaborative, creative, and high-stakes environments like PLC+ teams. The following steps outline how to activate these stages within your team's regular routines and conversations.

Approach	How to Activate
Inclusion Safety	Make sure every member feels welcomed and valued.
	Learn and use each other's names, listen actively, ask twice as much as you tell, and avoid competitive comparisons.
Learner Safety	Promote a growth mindset.
	Model vulnerability by sharing what you're learning and mistakes you've made, and invite others to do the same.
	Ask for feedback regularly.
Contributor Safety	Clarify team roles, and celebrate progress, including small wins.
	Encourage shared ownership of team goals and create an environment where input is expected, not optional.
Challenger Safety	Reward thoughtful risk-taking and respectful disagreement.
	Challenge ideas without blame or defensiveness, and make it safe to identify inefficiencies and speak truth to power.

SUCCESS CHECKLIST

✓	Activation Task
Note Potential Challenges	
☐	PLC+ team members rarely speak or seem hesitant to share ideas or concerns.
☐	Conversations are dominated by one or two voices, limiting diverse input.
☐	Team members avoid risk taking, disagreement, or open discussion of challenges.
Activate	
☐	Model vulnerability by admitting mistakes and asking for help or feedback in meetings.
☐	Create regular opportunities for all voices to be heard, such as structured protocols or turn-taking strategies.
☐	Affirm and celebrate contributions, especially when they reflect honest reflection, learning, or constructive challenge.
Reflect and Refine	
☐	How do team norms and behaviors support or hinder psychological safety?
☐	When was the last time someone challenged an idea in our team—and how was it received?
☐	What can I do as a leader or teammate to help others feel safe sharing openly?

Notes

41. TEAM DYNAMICS: ACTIVATING DIALOGUE WHEN TOPICS BECOME SENSITIVE

How do we keep our dialogue moving forward when working with sensitive topics where the focus easily shifts to blame, shame, and excuses?					
When					
	Before Meetings	✓	During Meetings		After Meetings
How Often					
	Planning	✓	Implementation		Reflection

Strategy in Action | Activating Dialogue When Topics Become Sensitive

qrs.ly/9kgpghs

STRATEGY-AT-A-GLANCE

When teams are discussing students and their learning, sensitive topics are likely to emerge. Efficient and effective teams have strategies to allow for the sensitive topics to be addressed. Strategies such as paraphrasing and questioning, validating and verifying, and keeping a clear focus on the outcome can help move the PLC+ forward.

RECOGNIZING THE NEED

The question about who did and who did not benefit from instruction can lead to difficult conversations. After a series of challenging meetings, one PLC+ participant observed: "There were times when we would avoid the obvious issue with our English language learners. We would stay on the surface, missing what was really going on. And when I tried to go deeper into the evidence, we would spiral into blaming parents, administrators, the central office … One day we even blamed the politicians. That was a tough day."

ACTIVATING WITH THIS STRATEGY

Most of us would agree that meaningful interaction requires some level of trust. But what is required when interactions move to sensitive topics? Your PLC+ may find that these sensitive conversations become difficult and unproductive. We've observed challenging discussions become superficial conversations that spiral into blame, shame, and excuses, while challenging even the most skilled activator's resolution skills. Consider these three strategies for activating the PLC+ team when dialogue stalls or retreats, so that you can push the PLC+ team toward effective discussions about growth and achievement.

Approach	How to Activate
Paraphrase and question.	During difficult conversations when blame and excuses permeate the PLC+ collaborative team meeting, activators can paraphrase the comments or side comments of colleagues and then ask a probing question. Focus the questions on helping colleagues differentiate between what they could and could not control.
Validate and verify.	When the dialogue in a PLC+ results in one member of the team making an assertion about individual students and their circumstances, activators can respond with a request that the comment be verified with the evidence. With time, others will engage in the same practice to ensure that the dialogue is evidence driven and not dictated by generalities and blame.
Keep a clear focus on the outcome.	At the start of each PLC+ team meeting, activators should provide a clear outcome for the meeting. Consider one that relates to who did and did not benefit from learning. If the dialogue seems to move off track, offer a "what if" scenario focused on the team members changing their instructional approach to benefit more students: *"What if we . . . ?"*

SUCCESS CHECKLIST

✓	Activation Task
	Note Potential Challenges
☐	Superficial conversations spiral into blame, shame, and excuses.
☐	The PLC+ team members make assertions about students without supporting evidence.
☐	The dialogue moves off track from determining who did and did not benefit from instruction.
	Activate
☐	Paraphrase colleagues' comments and ask probing questions to differentiate controllable factors.
☐	Request verification of assertions with evidence to maintain an evidence-driven dialogue.
☐	Provide a clear outcome for each meeting, and use "what if" scenarios to redirect discussions when collaboration strays away from the shared outcome.
	Reflect and Refine
☐	How has paraphrasing and questioning changed the tone of the discussion?
☐	How can evidence-based discussions positively impact team collaboration and the focus on student learning?
☐	What are ideal ways for outcomes to be optimized to best support the PLC+ team's collaboration and impact?

42. TEAM DYNAMICS: ACTIVATING WHEN TEAM MEMBERS DO NOT WANT TO CHANGE

How do we keep our PLC+ moving forward when it becomes clear that some (or most) team members do not want to change?					
When					
	Before Meetings	✓	During Meetings		After Meetings
How Often					
	Planning	✓	Implementation		Reflection

STRATEGY-AT-A-GLANCE

There are several reasons that individuals resist change. Maurer's (2010) three levels of resistance to change are *I don't get it, I don't like it,* and *I don't like you*. In the category *I don't get it*, resistance to change comes from not understanding the purpose of the change or how to change. Sometimes, resistance to change is more in the form of *I don't like it*, which is an emotional reaction. At other times, it's more about a lack of trust or confidence, as is the case in the category *I don't like you*. Regardless of the reason, activators need tools that allow them to address this resistance to change.

RECOGNIZING THE NEED

In their PLC+ meeting, the science teachers at Toloache Middle School share the following observations about their students: "You can see them disengage. Their body language sends a loud and clear message. They're closed off, and they avoid eye contact."

Ms. Munoz, the new PLC+ activator, reflects on the teachers' observations, "They don't have a good sense of why we need to change. In the past, the assessment data have been okay, not terrible, and not great, but good enough not to get noticed. Without understanding the purpose, we're probably not going to get anywhere, so I think we need to revisit that."

She begins to challenge the PLC+ team to think about the resistance she is seeing. She asks, "What would truly be necessary in terms of growth and change in our team's practice to better reach these students?"

ACTIVATING WITH THIS STRATEGY

Resistance is all but guaranteed to rise up in the PLC+ setting. Successful activators acknowledge this fact and prepare themselves in advance. They recognize that there are many types of resistance a PLC+ activator might encounter, all of which can challenge consensus and change. Informed by Maurer's levels (2010), activators can support the PLC+ team to effectively support dialogue and action that can support positive, predictable change in the face of a team member who is resistant.

Approach	How to Activate
Identify the reason for resistance. Then choose the appropriate response below based on the identified reason.	Listen and observe to develop a hypothesis: Is the resistance coming from *I don't get it, I don't like it,* or *I don't like you*? Importantly, resistance to change is a reaction to the way a change is being implemented. In other words, people resist in response to something—and understanding what is causing that resistance allows activators to build support for the ideas being generated.
If the resistance is due to *I don't get it*	This level involves the lack of information, disagreement about the interpretation of evidence, or perceptions of the value or purpose of the change. In response, activators can provide accurate information, allow for deeper analysis of the evidence, or revisit the purpose of the change and the rationale for engaging in the change.
If the resistance is due to *I don't like it*	This level is emotional; it involves participants' personal feelings about their skills to implement the change. In response, activators can address the emotions that are associated with the change or develop professional learning plans to build the skills of team members.
If the resistance is due to *I don't like you*	This level involves other people. The change is resisted due to a lack of trust or confidence in the person or people involved in the change. Sometimes, the people initiating the change are not part of the team. In response, activators can work on relational trust and invite the people involved in creating the change to share their reasons for the change.

SUCCESS CHECKLIST

✓	Activation Task
	Note Potential Challenges
☐	The PLC+ team shows resistance in body language (e.g., crossed arms, disengagement).
☐	High-performing teachers are reluctant to change.
☐	Long-time teachers who are comfortable with old methods do not see a reason to change or innovate.
	Activate
☐	Move forward without requiring full consensus.
☐	Connect PLC+ goals with daily classroom work.
☐	Break changes into small, manageable steps, and celebrate the achievement of each step—especially the first few, which will help the PLC+ gain momentum.
	Reflect and Refine
☐	What have you observed in terms of small changes that have led, or are leading, to larger shifts in practice?
☐	What is the role of collective efficacy in fostering change and ways to increase efficacy in your PLC+?
☐	How can you help team members understand the long-term benefits of incremental progress in your next PLC+ meeting?

Notes

43. TEAM DYNAMICS: ANALYZING AND DESCRIBING TEAM STRENGTHS

How do I identify and activate the unique strengths within my PLC+ team to build clarity, deepen collaboration, and drive continuous improvement?					
When					
	Before Meetings	✓	During Meetings		After Meetings
How Often					
	Planning	✓	Implementation		Reflection

Strategy in Action | Analyzing and Describing Team Strengths

qrs.ly/ytgpght

STRATEGY-AT-A-GLANCE

This strategy centers on identifying and leveraging the unique strengths within PLC+ teams to foster collaboration, clarity, and sustained impact. By analyzing each member's contributions and team dynamics, PLC+ teams can align their purpose, processes, communication, and impact with school-wide goals. This strengths-based approach enhances engagement, deepens trust, and equips teams to meet challenges with focus and cohesion.

RECOGNIZING THE NEED

At Meadowview Elementary, the fifth-grade PLC+ team gathers for its monthly collaboration. Ms. Carter, the reading specialist, expresses frustration that their initiatives aren't taking root, despite everyone working hard. Mr. Ramirez, the team lead, notices that decisions are often rushed and responsibilities unclear. Ms. Kim, a first-year teacher, quietly asks, "Do we really know what each of us brings to this team?" The room pauses as the team begins to wonder—are they missing the opportunity to understand and mobilize their individual and collective strengths?

ACTIVATING WITH THIS STRATEGY

Your strong PLC+ team will thrive on mutual respect, a shared vision, and a clear understanding of each member's unique contributions. Taking time to intentionally recognize strengths where they exist is a critical component of a thriving PLC+. This strategy recognizes that analyzing and describing team strengths is essential for building trust and fostering high-impact collaboration. Clarity in purpose, process, communication, and impact provides a framework for understanding and enhancing team effectiveness. By intentionally focusing on these areas, teams can harness their collective strengths to support continuous improvement and student success.

Approach	How to Activate
Clarity of Purpose	Reflect on what the team aims to achieve collectively and how each individual's skills, experiences, and values contribute to those shared goals. This includes articulating team commitments and aligning them with school-wide priorities.
Clarity of Process	Assess how decisions are made within the team and ensure that roles, responsibilities, and protocols are transparent and inclusive. Revisit whether all members feel empowered to contribute to planning and problem solving.
Clarity in Communication	Review expectations for how team members communicate with one another and with broader staff. Identify communication strengths and areas for improvement, ensuring consistency, transparency, and respect in all exchanges.
Clarity of Impact	Determine how the team will measure success, what tools will be used to collect and analyze data, and how results will be shared. Make impact visible by celebrating progress and tying actions to outcomes.
Use of Tools	Leverage surveys, team mapping exercises, and data from engagement assessments (many of which are available free of charge to schools) to surface patterns, name strengths, and identify opportunities for growth. These tools provide objective insights that support informed team development.
Leadership Support	Leaders should foster psychological safety, encourage vulnerability, and consistently recognize the contributions of team members. Facilitate regular, strengths-based check-ins, and ensure that all voices are heard in team conversations.

SUCCESS CHECKLIST

✓	Activation Task
	Note Potential Challenges
☐	There are signs of disengagement or unclear roles within the PLC+ team.
☐	Patterns in decision making either silence or overlook certain voices.
☐	Communication breakdowns affect follow-through or staff understanding.
	Activate
☐	Facilitate a team strengths inventory or reflection using structured prompts aligned to clarity of purpose, process, communication, and impact.
☐	Encourage team members to share and affirm each other's contributions in meetings.
☐	Revisit team commitments and refine processes based on an understanding of members' talents and preferences.
	Reflect and Refine
☐	What strengths do individual members bring to this PLC+ team, and how are they currently being used?
☐	In what ways do the team's processes and communication support or hinder collaboration?
☐	How can the group better align the team's strengths with the outcomes they hope to achieve for students and staff?

Notes

_____
_____
_____
_____
_____
_____
_____
_____
_____
_____
_____
_____

44. TEAM DYNAMICS: BREAKING BARRIERS, BRINGING TEAM MEMBERS TOGETHER

When conflict among team members challenges progress, should we go around, go over, or remove the barrier?					
When					
	Before Meetings	✓	During Meetings		After Meetings
How Often					
	Planning	✓	Implementation		Reflection

STRATEGY-AT-A-GLANCE

Generally speaking, there are five main causes of conflict: information conflicts, values conflicts, interest conflicts, relationship conflicts, and structural conflicts. As humans interact, a lack of common understanding, poor communication skills, unclear or unfair expectations, and power plays and manipulations create barriers between people. When the inability of one or more team members to get along arises, activators have the option to (a) go around, (b) go over, or (c) remove the barrier. This strategy will help you make an informed choice about how to address team member conflict.

RECOGNIZING THE NEED

During a PLC+ team meeting at the middle school, Mr. Salem, the science teacher, passionately defends hands-on labs as essential for student learning, while the math teacher, Ms. Lester, insists that structure and direct instruction are more effective. Their differing philosophies lead to tension as they struggle to find common ground. Disagreements continue to surface frequently, even over seemingly minor decisions like meeting agendas or assessment formats. Regardless of seeming minor, the barriers persistently limit the PLC+ team's progress and impact.

ACTIVATING WITH THIS STRATEGY

Looking around your PLC+ membership, it is likely that each individual team member strongly believes in the value of their specific content or way of teaching. As a result of these strongly held beliefs, you may reach a time when team members simply cannot get along. Despite shared goals for student success, strongly held individual beliefs about teaching can make collaboration challenging. When reaching this point, consider whether to go around, go over, or remove the barrier when synergy becomes challenged.

Approach	How to Activate
Approach PLC+ members individually.	To *go around* the barrier, we may decide to approach each of the members individually to engage in conversation about the intent and purpose of the PLC+ work and how each team member can contribute to this work. This one-on-one dialogue provides an opportunity for you and your colleague to gain a clearer perspective on the work.
Refocus the purpose.	To *get over* the barrier, we can devote a significant amount of time discussing the purpose of the PLC+ framework. During one meeting, an *activator* we know spent time reflecting with her colleagues about what PLC+ was and was not so that the collaborative team could refocus its purpose toward teaching and learning and away from comparisons between colleagues.
Clear the air.	To *remove* the barrier, you can allow colleagues to clear the air. This approach can be risky, but we should allow the conversation to unfold and simply redirect comments toward teaching and learning and away from personal attacks. Be prepared to involve other supports or mediation, if it comes to that, during efforts to clear the air.

SUCCESS CHECKLIST

✓	Activation Task
	Note Potential Challenges
☐	Team members strongly hold onto their specific beliefs about content or teaching.
☐	Disagreements extend beyond content into personal conflicts.
☐	There are signs that the PLC+ team is struggling to collaborate effectively.
	Activate
☐	Approach PLC+ members individually to engage in one-on-one conversations about the intent and purpose of PLC+ work.
☐	Devote time to discussing and refocusing the purpose of the PLC+ framework.
☐	Facilitate a structured discussion to clear the air and redirect conversations toward teaching and learning.
	Reflect and Refine
☐	Are personal biases involved in the conflict and, if so, how do they impact collaboration within the PLC+?
☐	What steps can you, as activator, take to ensure that the focus remains on student learning and away from personal differences?
☐	How can you help build trust, empathy, and perspective taking within the PLC+?

45. TEAM DYNAMICS: COUNTERING RESISTANCE WITH WILL, SKILL, KNOWLEDGE, CAPACITY, AND EMOTIONAL SUPPORT

How do I recognize and respond to the underlying causes of resistance in my PLC+ team in ways that build trust, support growth, and move learning forward?					
When					
	Before Meetings	✓	During Meetings		After Meetings
How Often					
	Planning	✓	Implementation		Reflection

STRATEGY-AT-A-GLANCE

Resistance is normal and can be a signal that we're ready for change. Resistance is the psychological term for *I don't want to do this!* As activators work with people who appear resistant, it is important to carefully assess the root cause of the challenge. This framework will help you recognize and consider the challenge and your abilities in the areas of will, skill, knowledge, capacity, and emotional support.

RECOGNIZING THE NEED

The room is quiet after the team reviews their latest assessment results.

"I'm starting to think I just don't know how to teach this standard differently," Mr. Alvarez admits, looking down at his notes. "I just can't think of any other way to have success with this content."

Without judgment, Ms. Kim offers, "Maybe it's not about having all the answers—we might just need to figure out where we're stuck and help each other from there."

Their activator, Mrs. Fields, leans in and says, "That's exactly the kind of moment where we pause, reflect, and decide together what needs to shift—starting with the support we need as professionals."

ACTIVATING WITH THIS STRATEGY

When resistance-related challenges with a PLC+ team member arise, ask yourself:

- "In what areas can I help this person?"
- "Where does this person struggle most?"
- "Where are their strengths?"

Then, acknowledge and call upon your activator abilities in each of the following areas.

Area	Affirmation
Will	You have the courage to take a risk in your zone of proximal development. The level of your commitment exceeds the fear and discomfort of the risk. You have the courage to engage this practice with diverse PLC+ members and in different settings.
Skill	You have practiced these skills extensively and are ready for a whole range of things that might happen. You know variations that can occur, can anticipate responses, and can get predictable results across settings when the conditions are all in place.
Knowledge	You have the declarative content knowledge to explain the theory and practice and to cite significant research and experience related to it. Note Potential Challenges: This does not mean you know, or need to know, everything.
Capacity	You have created the time and material support systems for you to practice and utilize your activator skills. You can find the time, organize the work, get the materials, prepare the conditions, and so on.
Emotional Support	You have built the alliances necessary to engage to provide emotional support. You have made sure that you get the emotional release you need to work with diverse groups and settings.

Source: Tool developed by the National Equity Project.

SUCCESS CHECKLIST

✓	Activation Task
	Note Potential Challenges
☐	There are signs of resistance, such as disengagement, defensiveness, or withdrawal from team discussions.
☐	Patterns in behavior point to underlying issues with will, skill, knowledge, capacity, or emotional support.
☐	Team members seem overwhelmed, underprepared, or unsupported in trying new practices.
	Activate
☐	Ask reflective questions to identify where a colleague is struggling and where they show strength.
☐	Match your support to the area of need—whether it's encouragement, resources, knowledge sharing, or collaboration.
☐	Revisit and activate your own strengths in will, skill, knowledge, capacity, and emotional support to model and guide the team.
	Reflect and Refine
☐	Are you providing the kind of support a colleague truly needs—or are you just providing the kind you're most comfortable giving?
☐	Which area (will, skill, knowledge, capacity, or emotional support) do you personally need to strengthen to better lead through resistance?
☐	How can you ensure that the team feels challenged and supported in moving through discomfort toward meaningful change?

Notes

46. TEAM DYNAMICS: FROM INDEPENDENT TO AN INTERDEPENDENT PLC+

How do I create a culture where PLC+ team members enjoy and come to rely upon interdependence?					
When					
Before Meetings	✓	During Meetings		After Meetings	
How Often					
Planning	✓	Implementation		Reflection	

STRATEGY-AT-A-GLANCE

Although your entire school may now be invested in the PLC+ framework, you and your colleagues may find that although you've been grouped together, you are still working independently on your instruction. A focus on collaboration, including understanding and pursuing interdependence among team members, will result in greater impact for the PLC+ effort. Understanding the need for collaboration, regularly discussing the benefits, and recognizing successes on the way to true interdependence all stand to directly benefit your PLC+ effort.

RECOGNIZING THE NEED

At the Tuesday PLC+ meeting, Ms. Ramirez glances around the table and asks, "Has anyone noticed we've all been here every week, but we're each still planning and analyzing data in isolation?"

Mr. Jacobs nods slowly and replies, "It's true—our students might be growing, but imagine what we could accomplish if we actually built on each other's strengths."

Dr. Nguyen, serving as the team's activator, chimes in by saying, "Let's start tracking how much of our time is spent truly collaborating versus working independently, and talk next week about how we can shift that balance."

Inspired, the team also agrees to visit a neighboring grade-level PLC+ known for strong interdependence and use that example to reshape their own approach.

ACTIVATING WITH THIS STRATEGY

We have seen teams gather around a table while members simply work on their "own thing." In some of these cases, particularly when the PLC+'s data indicate gains in student learning, it can be especially hard for the instructional leadership team to spark a change. In other cases, there are missed opportunities for increasing gains in student learning.

As an activator, watch for times when team interdependence becomes hard to find. Note when members are more focused on their own individual priorities and needs, rather than interacting with the PLC+ team. Here are four useful activation approaches that can move the PLC+ toward better, deeper, and more frequent collaboration.

Approach	How to Activate
Take note of collaboration.	Raise awareness of the team's collaboration levels as a starting point for increasing collaboration. Ask each team member to observe and monitor the amount of time dedicated to collaboration versus independent tasks and tasks that require little, if any, interdependence.
Capitalize on successes.	Ask the team to look for successful collaborations that have enhanced and enriched student learning. Then celebrate and share these successes across the school during faculty meetings, at professional development days, and through the daily announcements. Highlight the specific collaboration in each celebration.
Discuss the *what* and *why* of interdependence.	Celebrating the successes of a PLC+ is not enough. The activators of each PLC+ should spend additional time engaging members in a dialogue about interdependence—what it is and the value it affords when successfully present.
Model.	The instructional leadership team should embrace opportunities to model the interdependence expected during the PLC+ process. For example, members might visit and observe the iterative work of teaching teams across the building, followed by a discussion around interdependence examples they observed.

SUCCESS CHECKLIST

✓	Activation Task
	Note Potential Challenges
☐	PLC+ team meetings lack conversation.
☐	During PLC+ team meetings, not enough time is dedicated to shared conversation and tasks that require collaboration.
☐	Team members are not engaged in transforming tasks they pursue individually into opportunities to increase collaboration.
	Activate
☐	Share your observation with the PLC+ team when independent work is overshadowing collaboration and team interdependence.
☐	Define interdependence and its alignment with PLC+ outcomes. Discuss the benefits and limitations of individual work versus team collaboration and interdependence.
☐	Use storytelling to highlight times when the PLC+ effort has been propelled forward through collaboration and/or interdependence.
	Reflect and Refine
☐	Has the amount of time spent in collaboration vs independent work changed over time? Have team members taken note of the shift?
☐	Do PLC+ team members understand the what, why, and potential benefits of collaboration and interdependence?
☐	How can you continue to activate to greater interdependence using the approach or approaches that have proven successful?

Notes

TIME MATTERS

An Introduction to Time Matters
qrs.ly/a6gpghv

47. TIME MATTERS: DEVELOPING AN ASSESSMENT CALENDAR

How do we regularly integrate assessment data into our PLC+ meetings, with the right data being available and discussed at the right time?					
When					
✓	Before Meetings		During Meetings		After Meetings
How Often					
✓	Planning		Implementation		Reflection

Strategy in Action | Developing an Assessment Calendar

qrs.ly/krgpghy

STRATEGY-AT-A-GLANCE

Building an assessment calendar involves planning and scheduling when assessments and the data they generate will be available to your PLC+ team. Timing assessments so that they benefit your PLC+, including the team's instructional decisions, is key to establishing and maintaining a data-driven and data-informed effort. Planning your assessments, along with your meeting schedule, is a helpful exercise at the beginning of each year.

RECOGNIZING THE NEED

In a staff room discussion, Ms. Lopez frowns at the calendar in front of her and says, "We've got our PLC+ meetings planned, and we know our assessment schedule, but how are we supposed to make these work together?"

Mr. Chan nods in agreement, adding, "We need one unified plan—right now it's like trying to solve a puzzle with pieces from two different boxes."

Ms. Hernandez chimes in by adding, "Merging the assessment schedule into the PLC+ calendar will help us make sure our meetings actually use the data to move student learning forward."

With that, the team agrees to revise their schedule using the PLC+ framework to align data availability with strategic meeting topics and goals.

ACTIVATING WITH THIS STRATEGY

Using the PLC+ calendar you developed, add your assessment data plans to describe the administration and analysis of these assessments of learning. Keep in mind that you and your team may have to edit and revise your original calendar to accommodate assessment data, its analysis, and its use by the PLC+ team. After establishing the calendar at the beginning of the year, you should also revisit the assessment elements of your schedule following each infusion of data. The team can discuss how the most recent data benefited, and didn't benefit, the overall PLC+ effort. Based on the learnings surfaced here, consider any adjustments to your assessment schedule and then update your plan for the remainder of the year. Before designing an assessment calendar, let's review four types of assessments as described in the following summary table.

Type	Purpose	Time Span	Examples
Short-cycle assessments	Gauge student understanding during instruction to inform near-term instructional decisions.	Within and between lessons	Checks for understanding (e.g., exit tickets, universal response opportunities, questioning)
Medium-cycle assessments	Gauge student progress toward mastery of unit goals. May be used within or between units to make decisions about reteaching or extension and enrichment.	2–6 weeks	Practice tests, short constructed responses linked to unit goals or success criteria
Long-cycle assessments	Gauge student progress toward mastery of standards. Review curriculum alignment.	6–10 weeks or longer	Common formative items assessments within or across the building interim and benchmark assessments
Annual assessments	Measure mastery of standards. Screening measures.	Once a year	State assessments End-of-course competencies Screening inventories Diagnostic tests

Source: Adapted from Wiliam et al. (2024). *Student assessment: Better evidence, better decision, better learning* (Figure 2.1, p. 20). Corwin.

Short-cycle assessments, such as universal response opportunities, do not need to be calendared by the PLC+ team, as these are performed frequently throughout the lesson to make minute-by minute instructional decisions. However, *medium-cycle assessments* are especially useful on the team's calendar, as these consist of initial, midunit, and end-of-unit assessments. Therefore, they provide frequent data collection and analysis opportunities for the team to gauge their progress as it relates to the common challenge. *Long-cycle assessments* occur intermittently throughout the year and provide teams with further data across the year to make midcourse adjustments. Examples of these include district benchmark assessments; Lexile results; and commercial products used by the school, such as i-Ready and NWEA data, to measure growth and progress at the beginning, middle, and end of the year. A final item for the assessment calendar are those administrated *annually*. These include annual screenings and readiness assessments administered in the beginning of the year, language proficiency measures, as well as state assessments.

Assessment Types	Date of Assessments	Date Data Become Available

Now, assimilate your state, district, and local assessment calendar into your PLC+ meeting cycle. For example, the scheduled meeting for *"What did we learn today?"* may need to be moved in the meeting cycle so that this occurs after a medium-cycle assessment. Now, look at the example of an assessment calendar in the following table to imagine how your own list might look in context.

Month	Week of	Medium-Cycle Assessments (2–6 weeks)	Long-Cycle Assessments (6–10 weeks)	Annual Assessments
August	19			
	26	Unit 1 Initial Assessment		Math screening (results available 9/23)
September	2			Reading screening (results available 9/30)
	9	Unit 1 Post-Assessment	Lexile reading measure (Beginning of Year [BOY])	
	16	Unit 2 Initial Assessment	Math benchmark (BOY)	
	23			
	30			
October	7	Unit 2 Post-Assessment		
	14	Unit 3 Initial Assessment		
	21			
	28			

Month	Week of	Medium-Cycle Assessments (2–6 weeks)	Long-Cycle Assessments (6–10 weeks)	Annual Assessments
November	4	Unit 3 Post-Assessment		
	11	Unit 4 Initial Assessment		
	18			
	25			
December	2			
	9			
	16	Unit 4 Post-Assessment		
January	6	Unit 5 Initial Assessment		
	13		Lexile reading measures (Middle of Year [MOY])	
	20		Math benchmark (MOY)	District writing assessment (results returned March)
	27	Unit 5 Post-Assessment		
February	3	Unit 6 Initial Assessment		Language proficiency measure window begins (results available next fall)
	10			
	17			
	24			
March	2	Unit 6 Post-Assessment		
	9	Unit 7 Initial Assessment		
	16			
	23			
April	6			
	13		Lexile reading measures (End of Year [EOY])	
	20	Unit 7 Post-Assessment	Math benchmark (EOY)	
	27	Unit 8 Initial Assessment		
May	4			State testing window opens (results available next fall)
	11			
	18	Unit 8 Post-Assessment		
	25			

SUCCESS CHECKLIST

✓	Activation Task
Note Potential Challenges	
☐	Potential conflicts exist between meeting and assessment schedules.
☐	There are gaps in data availability that might delay decision making.
☐	The PLC+ team misses potentially beneficial patterns in assessment results because they have not scheduled time to give the data the immediate attention it requires.
Activate	
☐	Merge the meeting and assessment calendars into a final document.
☐	Conduct team discussions to reflect on data utility after each infusion.
☐	Adjust the plan to incorporate insights gained from recent assessments and to add any new assessments that are planned.
Reflect and Refine	
☐	How effectively do PLC+ meetings use assessment data to drive learning?
☐	Does the schedule support timely and actionable data analysis?
☐	What changes could improve the integration of assessments into PLC+?

Notes

48. TIME MATTERS: SCHEDULING PLC+ MEETINGS

What is the best way to schedule PLC+ meetings to maximize our time and other PLC+ investments such that we achieve the greatest impact?					
When					
✓	Before Meetings		During Meetings		After Meetings
How Often					
✓	Planning		Implementation		Reflection

Strategy in Action | Scheduling PLC+ Meetings

qrs.ly/pegpgi0

STRATEGY-AT-A-GLANCE

Strategic scheduling is a foundational driver of effective PLC+ work. This strategy encourages teams to create a thoughtful, year-long meeting plan that aligns with the PLC+ guiding questions, integrates values-based reflection, and allows space for flexibility and team autonomy. By intentionally structuring the flow of collaboration, teams can ensure purposeful dialogue, avoid repetitive cycles, and track their progress over time. This approach not only supports team clarity and commitment but also enhances momentum and sustainability across the school year.

RECOGNIZING THE NEED

During the third PLC+ meeting of the month, Mr. Weston glances around and asks, "Didn't we just talk about this last week?"

Ms. Navarro replies, "It feels like we're circling the same conversations without getting anywhere."

Their activator, Mr. Lane, takes a deep breath and says, "What we're missing is a roadmap—something that makes sure each meeting moves us forward."

From that point on, the team commits to building a schedule that balances structure with flexibility and clarity with purpose.

ACTIVATING WITH THIS STRATEGY

To implement this strategy, begin by cocreating a meeting schedule that reflects your team's availability, instructional calendar, and key PLC+ milestones. Be sure to include cycles that revisit each of the five PLC+ questions and integrate check-ins to monitor alignment with team goals and shared values. In year 1, it's helpful to maintain a more structured approach, with predetermined topics such as assessments, data analysis, and norm setting.

Build in reflection opportunities at regular intervals (e.g., "Now What?/So What?" sessions) to surface what's working, what's not, and what the team needs to learn next. These check-in points become vital indicators of momentum and inform midcourse corrections. To build collective efficacy, teams should also plan time to celebrate progress and accomplishments.

By year 2, PLC+ teams can assume more ownership over the scheduling process. Flexibility increases, but so does the importance of intentionality. Strong facilitation—paired with clear expectations and team autonomy—creates a sustainable rhythm that fuels continuous improvement.

The following table presents the plan for the first cycle of a team. There are many variations to the ways in which teams design their meeting schedule based on their experience as a group and the needs of their students.

Meeting Dates	Focus/Guiding Questions	Additional Recommendations
August 12	Initial Meeting	Start school year and establish role of PLC+, team focus, norms, and other essentials.
August 19	Questions 1, 2, and 3	Focus on students' strengths, analyze upcoming standards, and agree on evidence collection approaches.
August 26	Common Challenge	Based on students' strengths and knowledge of the standards for the year, identify a common challenge.
September 2	Questions 3 and 4	Decide on instructional approaches and what has been learned thus far.
September 9	Questions 5 and 2	Identify the benefits from the learning experiences and revisit student strengths.
September 16	Questions 3 and 5	Discuss the impact of instructional approaches and needed revisions to support students.
September 23	Questions 4 and 5	Analyze evidence and identify who benefited from the experiences.
September 30	Revisit common challenge and identify next challenge	Determine the progress made on the common challenge, celebrate successes, and revise the challenge or develop a new challenge.

SUCCESS CHECKLIST

✓	Activation Task
	Note Potential Challenges
☐	Repetitive discussions lack direction or forward momentum.
☐	There are unclear or inconsistent meeting goals across sessions.
☐	The team is uncertain about which PLC+ question is being addressed in a given meeting.
	Activate
☐	Develop a schedule that integrates all five PLC+ guiding questions and allocates time for values check-ins and reflections.
☐	Include "Now What?/So What?" meetings in the schedule to assess impact and identify adult learning needs.
☐	Support the team in gradually transitioning to more autonomous scheduling while maintaining clear purpose and consistency.
	Reflect and Refine
☐	How does the team's current meeting schedule support or hinder meaningful collaboration?
☐	Is the team using their time strategically to support teacher learning and student outcomes?
☐	What adjustments could help the team ensure that each meeting builds on the last and drives continuous improvement?

Notes

_____
_____
_____
_____
_____
_____
_____
_____
_____
_____
_____

49. TIME MATTERS: SETTING ASIDE TIME FOR THE PLC+

How do we make sure the time allocated to our PLC+ work is sufficient for success?					
When					
✓	Before Meetings		During Meetings		After Meetings
How Often					
✓	Planning		Implementation		Reflection

Strategy in Action | Setting Aside Time for PLC+

qrs.ly/mcgpgi3

STRATEGY-AT-A-GLANCE

Time is one of the most valuable resources a PLC+ team can protect. This strategy highlights the need to set aside time intentionally for inquiry, collaboration, and reflection. Whether meeting weekly or more frequently, teams benefit from planning ahead and safeguarding that time. A well-balanced schedule that includes learning, data review, and values check-ins strengthens impact and sustainability. Prioritizing collaborative time builds momentum that supports growth for students and educators.

RECOGNIZING THE NEED

"I thought this was the meeting about writing rubrics," Ms. Alvarez says, tapping her pen against her notebook as the conversation meanders.

Mr. Hobbs sighs and says, "We've been orbiting the same ideas for fifteen minutes and haven't landed on anything useful."

Without a word, Ms. Patel, the team's activator, wheels her chair to the whiteboard and draws a clean, simple calendar. She smiles and says, "Let's stop drifting and chart our course—our time should lift our students, not get lost in the fog."

From that moment on, the team commits to planning with clarity and purpose.

ACTIVATING WITH THIS STRATEGY

We have had the pleasure of working with many schools and districts that have found efficient and effective ways of activating the PLC+ framework and leveraging the four crosscutting values within their time frames. What follows are examples that serve as guides for making it work. Specifically, these strategies are from teams during their first two years of activating a PLC+.

Approach	How to Activate
Annual Calendar Planning	Start by mapping out your PLC+ calendar for the year, identifying consistent meeting times and setting expectations for attendance, preparation, and participation. Include key dates for values check-ins, assessment reviews, and investigation cycle reflections.
Prioritize Structure in Year 1	In the first year, emphasize structure over spontaneity. Ensure that time is allocated for every phase of the investigation cycle and build in regular "Now What?/So What?" reflection points to evaluate progress and identify learning needs.
Streamline for Time	Streamline processes while maintaining focus on the core elements of PLC+. Short, well-planned meetings can yield strong outcomes. Rotate roles and build routines to make efficient use of every session.
Protect Collaborative Space	Setting aside time is not just a logistical task—it reflects a professional commitment to collective growth. Protecting this time helps ensure that the conditions necessary for sustained, meaningful improvement in teaching and learning are implemented effectively.

SUCCESS CHECKLIST

✓	Activation Task
	Note Potential Challenges
☐	The PLC+ team engages in unfocused or repetitive meetings without clear direction or purpose.
☐	Inconsistent attendance or preparation undermines team momentum.
☐	The team misses opportunities for reflection or values-based discussion due to time constraints.
	Activate
☐	Create and share an annual PLC+ calendar with consistent meeting times and key task dates.
☐	Prioritize structure in Year 1 to ensure that all phases of the inquiry cycle are addressed.
☐	Use short, focused meetings with rotating roles and reinforce routines and protocols.
	Reflect and Refine
☐	How well is the team protecting their collaborative time, and how is it impacting their work?
☐	Are the PLC+ meetings strategically scheduled to support student and teacher learning?
☐	What small changes to the PLC+ schedule or meeting structure could help the team use the time more effectively?

REFLECTING ON YOUR ACTIVATION OF THE PLC+ JOURNEY

50. METAREFLECTION AND INTENTION SETTING WITH THE 5Ds

We've covered a lot of ground! With forty-nine strategies available and now familiar, we trust that your ideas and inspirations for activating your PLC+ are freely flowing. Keep this guide by your side, and call upon the strategies regularly—note when things are moving forward and why they are, and consult the guide when help is needed to accomplish the same.

We'll close this guide with Strategy 50—an opportunity for reflection. Perhaps better said, this is an invitation for metareflection because you'll be reflecting across the PLC+ strategies and journey. It really doesn't matter whether you are just beginning, are knee deep, or are quite accomplished with activation. Take fifteen to thirty minutes to reflect on where you'll go next by making your intentions, aspirations, and actions concrete.

USING THE 5Ds

We'll use the 5Ds to scaffold your metareflection. The 5D framework, first defined by Hamilton and colleagues (2022), supports turning your ideas into goals and then turning those goals into impact. It presents five elements that together define the implementation of a program, initiative, or journey. From Discover to Double Up a successful program, the five elements serve as a helpful organizing and ideating tool.

Use the table that follows to record your current thinking in the following two areas:

1. Your current thinking—including what you've learned about PLC+ and activation thus far and how you've used it.

2. Your intentions and aspirations—where you plan to go next in activating your PLC+ journey, including concrete steps you want to take and the timeline on which you're committing to do so.

PLC+ Activation Metareflection and Intention Setting

5D	Description	What You've Learned and Accomplished Thus Far	Intentions for Future Effort	Date for Realizing Each Intention
Discover . . .	The PLC+ model, what it means to be an activator, the skills you'll apply in this role, and the activator's criticality in the PLC+ model			

5D	Description	What You've Learned and Accomplished Thus Far	Intentions for Future Effort	Date for Realizing Each Intention
Design . . .	Your PLC+ work—from understanding the strengths and needs of the team to setting your focus and creating a PLC+ plan that returns results for your team, your students, and your school community			
Deliver . . .	Your PLC+ plan's implementation—anticipating successes and barriers, strategies for midcourse modification or correction, turning conflict into connection, knowing it's time to return to Design			
Double Back . . .	To evaluate the implementation and impact of your work, guided by the PLC+ plan and outcomes, assessing the effectiveness of the activator and team contributions, and using the results to inform refining or recasting the work			
Double Up . . .	By using strategies for sustaining your PLC+ effort by embedding it in the culture of your team and school, embracing continuous improvement, and maintaining focus through tangible goals that may shift, with team consensus over time			

SUCCESS CHECKLIST

✓	Activation Task
	Note Potential Challenges
☐	There are signs of stagnation in the PLC+ cycle, such as repetitive conversations or lack of focus.
☐	There are gaps between planned actions and actual outcomes in the current PLC+ implementation.
☐	There are overlooked opportunities to share success or scale practices across additional teams or schools.
	Activate
☐	Use the 5Ds framework to document what you've discovered, designed, and delivered so far in your PLC+ journey.
☐	Set intentions using the Double Back and Double Up stages to refine your approach and expand your reach.
☐	Schedule a reflection session with your team to review past strategies and cocreate plans for future activation.
	Reflect and Refine
☐	How has your understanding of the activator role evolved since the team began the PLC+ journey?
☐	What barriers or breakthroughs have shaped the team's implementation, and how will you respond going forward?
☐	What does sustainable PLC+ activation look like in your context, and what support will you need to achieve it?

REFERENCES

Bandura, A. (1997). *Self-efficacy: The exercise of control.* W. H. Freeman.

Clark, T. (2020). *The 4 stages of psychological safety.* Berrett-Koehler Publishers, Inc.

Costa, A. L., & Garmston, R. J. (2015). *Cognitive coaching: Developing self-directed leaders and learners* (3rd ed.). Rowman & Littlefield.

Edmondson, A. (2018). *The fearless organization: Creating psychological safety in the workplace for learning, innovation, and growth.* John Wiley & Sons.

Eells, R. (2011). *Meta-analysis of the relationship between collective efficacy and student achievement.* Unpublished doctoral dissertation. Loyola University of Chicago.

Engel, M., Claessens, A., Watts, T., & Farkas, G. (2016). Mathematics content coverage and student learning in kindergarten. *Educational Researcher, 45*(5), 293–300.

Fisher, D., & Frey, N. (2025). *Your introduction to PLC+: Building collaborative teams that drive student success.* Corwin.

Garmston, R. J. (2012). *Unlocking group potential to improve schools.* SAGE.

Garmston, R. J., & Wellman, B. M. (2016). *The adaptive school: A sourcebook for developing collaborative groups* (3rd ed.). Rowman & Littlefield.

Hamilton, A., Reeves, D. B., Clinton, J. M., & Hattie, J. (2022). *Building to impact: The 5D implementation playbook for educators.* Corwin.

Heron, J. (1999). *The complete facilitators handbook.* Kogan Page.

Hirsch, S. (2010). Collective responsibility makes all teachers the best. *Teachers Teaching Teachers.* https://learningforward.org/docs/leading-teacher/sept10_hirsch.pdf?sfvrsn=2

Hord, S. M. (1980). *Working together: Cooperation or collaboration?* The Research and Development Center for Teacher Education, University of Texas at Austin.

Lawrence, M. (2017). *Red sister.* Ace Books.

Levi, D. (2014). *Group dynamics for teams* (4th ed.). SAGE.

MacDonald, E. (2023). *How skillful team leaders impact learning.* Corwin.

Marshall, J. (2023). *Right from the start: The essential guide to implementing school initiatives.* Corwin.

Marshall, J. (2024). *Fixing education initiatives in crisis: 24 go-to strategies.* Corwin.

Maurer, R. (2010). *Beyond the wall of resistance* (2nd ed.). Bard Press.

Prenger, R., Poortman, C. L., & Handelzalts, A. (2019). The effects of networked professional learning communities. *Journal of Teacher Education, 70*(5), 441–452.

Senge, P., Cambron-McCabe, N., Lucas, T., Smith, B., & Dutton, J. (2012). *Schools that learn: A fifth discipline fieldbook for educators, parents, and everyone who cares about education* (2nd ed.). Crown Business.

Spiro, J. (2012). Winning strategy: Set benchmarks of early success to build momentum for the long term. *Journal of Staff Development, 33*(2), 10–16.

Sylwester, R. (1994). How emotions affect learning. *Educational Leadership, 52*(2), 60–65.

Szulanski, G. (1996). Exploring internal stickiness: Impediments to the transfer of best practices within the firm. *Strategic Management Journal, 17,* 27–43. https://doi.org/10.1002/smj.4250171105

Venables, D. R. (2011). *The practice of authentic PLCs: A guide to effective teacher teams.* Corwin.

Wang, N., & An, B. G. (2023). Improving teachers' professional development through professional learning community: Voices from secondary school teachers at Malaysian Chinese independent schools. *Heliyon, 9*(6), e17515–e17515. https://doi.org/10.1016/j.heliyon.2023.e17515

Wasik, B. A., & Hindman, A. H. (2018). Why wait? The importance of wait time in developing young students' language and vocabulary skills. *Reading Teacher, 72*(3), 369–378.

Wiliam, D., Fisher, D., & Frey, N. (2024). *Student assessment: Better evidence, better decisions, better learning.* Corwin.

INDEX

Activating questions, PLC+ Model, 5
   "How do we move learning forward?" 26–29
   "What did we learn today?" 30–33
   "Where are we going?" 16–19
   "Where are we now?" 20–25
   "Who benefitted and who did not benefit?" 34–37

Activator skills and abilities, 5
   evidence-based practices, 40
   fitness level, 42–45
   grace quality, 58–59
   key activator, finding, 60–63
   learning impact, 40–41
   PLC+ teams, success of, 40, 50–54
   role, 46–49
   self-assessment, 54–57

Active listening, 11, 55, 59, 142, 144, 146
Adaptive leadership, 10, 74
Adult learning, 50–52, 142, 206
Annual assessments, 199–201
Artifacts, 10, 103
Artificial intelligence (AI), 115, 116

Clark, T., 172
Cognitive coaching, 11, 142, 150
Cognitive Coaching (Costa and Garmston), 6
Coherence, 12, 74
Collective effervescence, 7, 8
Collective efficacy, 8, 10, 11, 95, 96, 158, 180, 205
Collective responsibility, 7–8
Continuous improvement, 5, 9–10, 51
   course corrections, 70–73
   discussions and actions, 66–69
   practices to scale, 74–77
   team structures, high level, 78–79
Costa, A. L., 146, 150

Credibility, 4, 42, 43, 50, 52, 159
Crosscutting values, 2, 3, 9, 126, 208

Data collection, 155, 199
Data conversation, 11, 60
Disaggregated data, 9, 91
Distress-free authority, 58–59
Distributed leadership, 10, 52, 60, 75, 109

Edmondson, A., 172
Empathy, 58, 59, 134, 187
Equity, 9, 56, 95, 118–119
Evaluative thinking, 10, 86–89
Evidence-based instructional approach, 2, 9, 40, 41, 95
Evidence-informed cycles, 11, 66, 102

Fisher, D., 2
5Cs (clarity, consciousness, competence, confidence, and credibility) framework, 42–44
5Ds (discover, design, deliver, double back, and double up) framework, 212–214
Frey, N., 2
Function and impact, PLC+, 5, 10
   current performance level, 94–99
   early momentum building, 100–101
   evaluation, work and success, 102–105
   evaluative thinking, 86–89
   optimal combination, 108–109
   readiness, 90–94
   sharing, story and success, 82–85
   student learning, 106–107

Garmston, R. J., 42, 122, 146, 150
Goal setting, 8, 10, 78, 79
Growth mindset, 9, 173

Hamilton, A., 212
Heron, J., 58
Hord, S. M., 90, 92

Inclusion, 9, 11, 56, 172, 173
Individualized Education Programs (IEPs), 146
Inquiry cycles, 10, 50, 86, 87, 139, 209
Instructional protocols, 11, 136–139

Lawrence, M., 2
Learning intentions, 9, 16–18, 20, 27, 34, 95
Levi, D., 127
Liberatory design, 3, 9, 10, 11, 12, 155
Long-cycle assessments, 199–201

MacDonald, E., 78, 106, 108
Marshall, J., 82, 86
Maurer, R., 178, 179
Medium-cycle assessments, 199–201
Meeting moves, PLC+ establishment, 5, 10–11
    assessments and data, 130–133
    authentic instructional protocols, 136–139
    challenging moments, 118–121
    documentation and note-taking, 114–117
    norms, 122–125
    professional learning agreement, 112–113
    roles, 126–129
    social emotional check-ins, 134–135
Metareflection, 12, 212–214

Neutral language, 11, 158, 159
Norms of collaborative work, 6, 11, 79, 103
    conversational spaces, 142–145
    emotions, 162–165
    establishing, PLC+, 122–125
    ideas, 158–161
    paraphrasing, 146–149
    posing questions, 150–153
    positive intentions, 166–169
    qualitative and quantitative data, 154–157

Open-ended questions, 150, 152, 155

Paraphrasing, 146–149
Pausing in conversations, 142–145
Person-activator match, 61
PLC+ Model, 3–4, 3 (figure), 212
    activation goal, 7–8
    categories, eight, 5–7
    cycles, 9, 61, 67, 214
    evolution, 2
    leadership role, 5
    See also Function and impact, PLC+
Professional learning communities (PLCs), 1–2
Psychological safety, 6, 9, 11, 54, 134, 159, 172–175, 183
Purpose-driven protocol, 11, 137

Readiness assessment, 10, 90, 200
Real-time data, 10, 79
Red Sister (Lawrence), 2
Reframing, 40, 86, 166–169
Resilience, 4, 50–52
Respect for people, 58, 59

Scaling, 10, 74–76
Self-assessment, 9, 54–57, 95–97
Sensitive topics, 176–177
Shared leadership, 9, 78, 79
Shared vision, 10, 182
Short-cycle assessments, 199
Social cohesion, 142, 162, 163, 167
Social emotional check-ins, 11, 134–135
Social sensitivity, 11, 163
Specific, Measurable, Achievable, Relevant, Time-bound (SMART), 79
Spiro, J., 100
Stakeholders, 10, 87, 88, 127, 158
Storytelling, 10, 75, 76, 194
Strengths-based check-ins, 9, 11, 183
Structured check-ins, 66, 134
Success criteria, 9, 16–18, 20, 26, 27, 34, 95, 199
Sylwester, R., 58
Szulanski, G., 82

Team dynamics, 6, 11, 50
    barriers breaking, 186–187
    dialogues with sensitive topics, 176–177
    interdependence, 192–195

psychological safety, 172–173
resistance causes, 188–191
strengths, PLC+ team, 182–185
team members, 178–181
Timeline, PLC+, 6, 12
allocated time, 208–209
assessment data, 198–203
PLC+ meetings scheduling, 204–207
Triangulation, 10, 131
Trust building, 6, 11, 43, 50–53, 106, 107, 132, 134, 212

Wait time, 11, 142, 143
Wellman, B. M., 42, 122
Winning strategy, 83, 100–101, 103, 104

Your Introduction to PLC+ (Fisher and Frey), 2, 3, 7, 90, 126, 136, 138
assessment tool, 97–99
cross-reference table, 9–12
needs assessment tool, 91–92, 91 (figure)
self-assessment tool, 95–96 (figure)

Take your teaching further

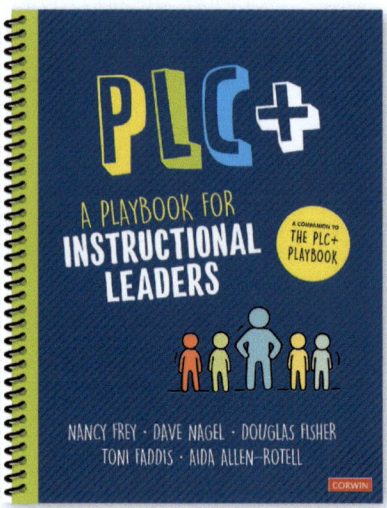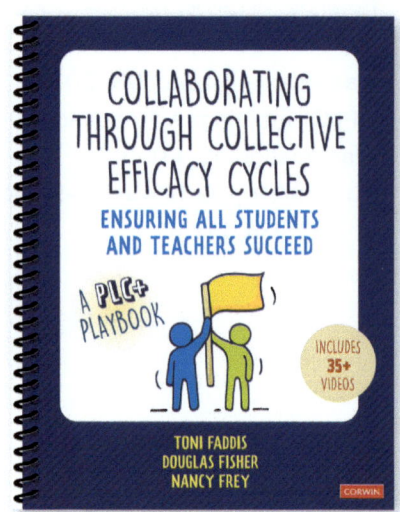

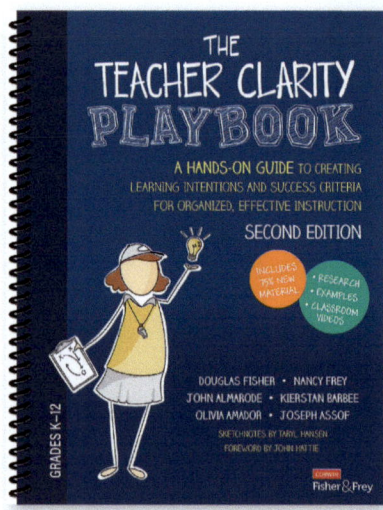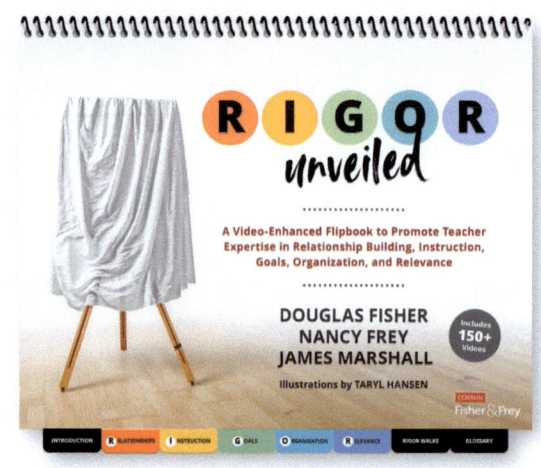

You may also be interested in...

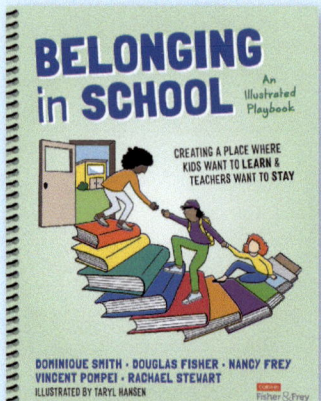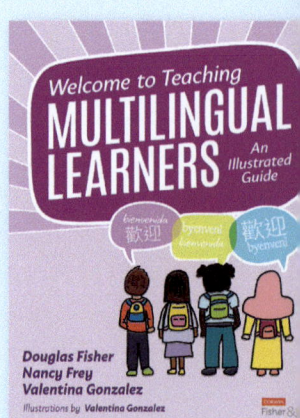

To learn more, visit corwin.com

Put your learning into practice

When you're ready to take your learning deeper, begin your journey with our PD services. Our personalized professional learning workshops are designed for schools or districts who want to engage in high-quality PD with a certified consultant, measure their progress, and evaluate their impact on student learning.

CORWIN PLC+

Empower teacher teams to build collective agency and remove learning barriers

It's not enough to just build teacher agency, we must also focus on the power of the collective. Empowering your PLCs is a step toward becoming better equipped educators with greater credibility to foster successful learners.

Get started at corwin.com/plc

CORWIN Teacher Clarity

Students learn more when expectations are clear

As both a method and a mindset, Teacher Clarity allows the classroom to transform into a place where teaching is made clear. Learn how to explicitly communicate to students what they will be learning on a given day, why they're learning it, and how to know if they were successful.

Get started at corwin.com/teacherclarity

CORWIN Visible Learning

Translate the science of how we learn into practices for the classroom

Discover how learning works and how this translates into potential for enhancing and accelerating learning. Learn how to develop a shared language of learning and implement the science of learning in schools and classrooms.

Get started at corwin.com/visiblelearning

Experience the Corwin Difference.
Learn more at corwin.com/the-corwin-difference

CORWIN

To help every educator help every student

We believe   that every single student deserves a great education

We believe   that knowing our impact is both a privilege and a responsibility

We believe   that a fair, stable, and thriving society is built on education